"The authors call for a new kind of spiritual leadership that reaches across generations, lifestyles, and cultures to advance the church's mission. Their vision takes the profound differences of age, race, and attitudes that so threaten many churches today and reframes them as potential strengths for the church and the world."

—Lovett H. Weems Jr., Distinguished Professor of Church Leadership, Wesley Theological Seminary, Washington, DC; coauthor with Tom Berlin, *High Yield: Seven Disciplines of the Fruitful Leader* and *Overflow: Increase Worship Attendance and Bear More Fruit*

"Get ready to be inspired, to move from a place of comfort, to be disrupted. *Blank Slate* shows us why generational behaviors and actions occur, and helps us dismiss preconceived ideas about people of all ages. It guides churches to discard our old rules and to develop new ones specifically for our congregation and community. This book will ultimately motivate people to engage with others in new ways, resulting in fuller, richer, and more meaningful ministry."

—Olu Brown, lead pastor, Impact Church, Atlanta, GA; author, *Leadership Directions from Moses* and *4D Impact: Smash Barriers Like a Smart Church*

"In a time when so many of us want a blueprint on how to do ministry in a rapidly changing world, McIntosh, Smothers, and Smothers hand us a pencil and tell us to draw it ourselves. *Blank Slate* reminds us that there is no cookie-cutter approach to moving the church into a dynamic new age. God has entrusted us to be the designers and visionaries for a new way. We have needed a book that looks ahead, a book that breaks down old barriers that

have held us back. This is that book. *Blank Slate* is the guide that you and your team need to design a new future together."

—Jacob Armstrong, pastor, Providence United Methodist Church, Mt. Juliet, TN; author, *The New Adapters*

"McIntosh, Smothers, and Smothers have told the truth on all of us. The truth really can set us free. They have perceptively and creatively invited us to *be church*, which is always to authentically commend the eternal gospel of Jesus Christ to ever-changing culture. Wake up, everybody."

—Gregory Vaughn Palmer, resident bishop, Ohio West Episcopal Area, United Methodist Church

"Three respected pastors provide data, keen observations, and a design process to assist leaders who long to create a multigenerational, multicultural, and innovative church. *Blank Slate* will help you see the world around you through a fresh lens."

—Tom Berlin, lead pastor, Floris United Methodist Church, Herndon, VA; coauthor with Lovett H. Weems Jr., *High Yield: Seven Disciplines of the Fruitful Leader* and *Overflow: Increase Worship Attendance and Bear More Fruit*

"I would encourage all lay persons, pastors, and judicatory leaders to engage this book. Don't just read it but *engage* it so that we might see a new movement of God's spirit through the church. These authors are 'on the money' with their analysis of our current cultural and church reality. They provide some great hints as to how we might move forward and become more relevant to our very diverse world."

—Robert Farr, bishop, Missouri Episcopal Area, United Methodist Church

Lia McIntosh
Jasmine Rose Smothers
Rodney Thomas Smothers

BLANK SLATE

Write Your Own Rules for a
22nd-Century Church Movement

Abingdon Press
Nashville

CONTENTS

Introduction

AN OPEN LETTER TO THE CHURCH

Millennial: Dear Baby Boomers, Thank you for all you've done, but I don't want your church.

Baby Boomer: What? You're not coming to church Sunday?

Millennial: Ummm, idk. [I don't know]

Baby Boomer: Why? I thought you loved this church. We miss you. We need you to keep the church going. You're supposed to replace us. We're tired.

Millennial: I love you, our relationship, but not your church... not the way you do it.

Baby Boomer: But we've always done it this way.

Millennial: Uh. Right. I know.

Baby Boomer: You don't believe in Jesus?

Millennial: I didn't say that...

Grandparents bemoan and parents are bugged because their Generation X, Millennial, and Generation Z children and grandchildren refuse to "inherit" their churches. This experience is common in many churches in the United States today. A recent survey of thirty-five thousand Americans by the

Pew Research Center confirmed that a rise of the "nones" has grown to encompass 23 percent of America's adults as of 2015.[1] This means that about one out of every four adults in the United States, when asked about their religious identity, would say "nothing." Further, many who were once in the church are now leaving it. About 19 percent of Americans, or 46 million adults, would call themselves "former" Christians. And, the generation being shaped most significantly by this, Generation Z, may come to represent the new reality of a majority post-Christian United States. Generation Z, youths born between 1995 and 2010, are roughly ages ten to twenty-five at the time of this writing. As the first mostly non-Christian generation, and numerically the largest, some researchers like James Emery White in his book titled *Meet Generation Z: Understanding and Reaching the New Post-Christian World* believes "Generation Z will be the most influential religious force in the U.S. and the heart of the missional challenge facing the Christian church."[2]

Rev. Dr. Leonard Sweet, futurist and scholar in American culture, in a presentation on how culture finds identity, names the decline in religious affiliation as a problem of reproduction. The faith of grandparents and parents is neither passed on to, nor embraced by, Millennials and younger generations. So doing church the way we've always known it is at risk of extinction. Dr. Sweet invites us to Google the phrase "Why are Christians so…"[3] When we try this exercise using Google, words like negative and judgmental, repulsive, sick, and hypocritical pop up. This reminds us of the current perceptions of some people toward the church. Beyond denominational tradition, worship style, or biblical in-terpretation, if there is not a deep understanding of, and love for, younger generations along with a willingness to transform their cultures, then churches, seminaries, and related organizations will not fulfill their mission.

In the tribe of which we are a part, The United Methodist Church, the average number of people who attend weekly worship (collected from over thirty thousand churches in the United States) has declined from 3,612,477 in 1972 to 2,659,427 in 2016. That is a decline of nearly one million people (26 percent) over the course of forty-four years.[4] If this trend continues, as it has over the past four decades across many American Christian denominations, the survival of individual brick-and-mortar congregations and the denomination as we know it is in jeopardy. This is not a new phenomenon. In 1776, John Wesley, the founder of the Methodist movement, wrote one of his most-quoted lines, "I am not afraid that the people called Methodists should ever cease to exist either in Europe or America. But I am afraid, lest they should only exist as a dead sect, having the form of religion without the power."[5]

So why are young adults, the most diverse generations in America, so difficult to reach by the traditional mainline church? And what can we do about it? In this book we'll attempt to answer these questions and provide recommendations to make your ministry more effective.

In sections 1 and 2, we'll look at the "old rules" of mature generations (Traditionalists, Boomers, and Generation X) and contrast them with the "new rules" of Millennials and Generation Z while shattering the myth that generations or microgenerations are monolithic. In fact, we've come to understand that demographics are fluid and lifestyles are constantly changing within and across generations. For example, MissionInsite, a demographic analysis tool, incorporates consumer lifestyle segmentation to understand and anticipate behaviors, attitudes, and preferences of the U. S. population. MissionInsite includes seventy-one Unique Individual Household Portraits and nineteen Overarching Groups.[6] Its mission is helping organizations become more mission-driven and sustainable (by understanding people better), attract more committed donors and volunteers, and then experience growth in impact and size. Notice that growth in size is an outcome of being mission-driven and deeply invested in people. Growth, in and of itself, is not the goal.[7] Deeper discipleship, relationships, and impact must be the first focus of any church, not its own institutional survival.

In this section, we will discuss differences across generations to build understanding. Yet, we also invite you to think across generations and lifestyles, and about people as one body instead of independent individuals, connected instead of autonomous, and interrelated instead of isolated. Theologians Michael O. Emerson, Curtiss Paul DeYoung, George Yancy, and Karen Chai Kim in their book *United by Faith: The Multiracial Congregation As an Answer to the Problem of Race* name this as a "theology of oneness" and make a case for multiracial congregations. Considering biblical, historical, and sociological perspectives, they argue against the common justifications for maintaining racially or ethnically distinct congregations and call for a new "theology of oneness." We support this understanding of God, while also recognizing that there is ample room in the church tent for distinct cultures while maintaining a "theology of oneness." Importantly, accepting the status quo of church decline, generational isolation, and cultural division is not sufficient. Use this section as a tool to help accelerate understanding, relational ability, theological discernment, and impact of your church.

In section 3, we'll highlight some of our favorite innovative organizations in the United States (Facebook, Starbucks, Uber, Netflix, and Disney) that are demonstrating deep understanding, relational ability, and impact with younger generations. Millennials are the least churched adult generation and the least likely either to identify as Christian or to say faith is very important to their life.[8] As a result, looking outside the church for understanding and effective strategy is essential.

As we stop, look, and listen a deeper question before the church is one of relevance across generations and cultures. To say something is relevant is to say it is meaningful and needed to achieve a purpose. If something is relevant it matters in the context of people's everyday lives. Businesses want their products to be relevant. Universities want their degree offerings to be relevant. Legislators want their laws to be relevant. Social media followers want their posts to be relevant. Nonprofits want their missions to be relevant. Preachers want their sermons to be relevant. We all want to believe that our work is relevant within today's society. We want to know that we matter. And churches must continually question their relevance to their customers if it is to stay in business. Often we don't want to think of churches as businesses. Yet, a central premise in this book is that business is simply an "appointed task" that must be relevant to others for viability. A business (whether for-profit or nonprofit) must be able to articulate WHY it matters for its customers or constituents today. Importantly, relevance is not just aspirational, it must be supported by data from people who give of their time, talents, financial gifts, and witness to others about the product or for the mission. We believe learning from innovative organizations like

Facebook, Starbucks, Uber, Netflix, and Disney can accelerate our understanding, relational ability, and impact of the church.

In section 4, we'll dive into the "blank slate." We've chosen the metaphor of a "blank slate" because it comes from the word *tabula rasa* meaning, "the mind in its hypothetical primary blank or empty state before receiving outside impressions."[9] We are all born with a blank slate, meaning that at birth, all humans are born with the ability to become anything or anyone. Yet, our life experiences and socialization impact who and what we actually become. Likewise, if we can strip away previous assumptions, fears, and cultural stereotypes, we can shift mindsets, create new experiences, and shape the future of the church no matter what the current state. We'll invite you into a blank slate using design thinking as a model to create innovative solutions to problems while putting the people you're trying to reach at the center.

In particular, for organizations that are service based, like the church, design thinking is all about creating remarkable experiences with Millennials and Generation Z at the center, because these are the younger generations we seek to reach. In today's world the best organizations are shifting from just providing services to creating memorable experiences. As a result, organizations that were once commodities-focused are differentiating themselves, growing profits, and connecting with new generations.

Spiritually, as Paul commands the church in Ephesians 4:20-24, this blank slate is an entirely new way of life:

> …You learned Christ! My assumption is that you have paid careful attention to him, been well instructed in the truth precisely as we have it in Jesus. Since, then, we do not have the excuse of ignorance, everything—and I do mean everything—connected with that old way of life has to go. It's rotten through and through. Get rid of it! And then take on an entirely new way

of life—a God-fashioned life, a life renewed from the inside and working itself into your conduct as God accurately reproduces his character in you.[10]

With this blank slate, the kind of action we're calling for is a new kind of spiritual leadership that reaches across generations, lifestyles and cultures. Importantly, this kind of leadership is the call of every person, not just religious professionals. In the role of spiritual leader a person chooses to be immersed in the world and in God. She loves humanity and Jesus. He seeks diverse relationships with people and deliberately takes time away from people to be with God. This leader is led by a deep knowing that the pandemonium of life does not have the last word. This new spiritual leader realizes that we are courageously living in between times of sadness and joy, turmoil and peace, disbelief and eternal hope. Importantly, at our best, spiritual leaders bear their souls through the sharing of personal struggles so others may see the enduring qualities of God, experience courage and remain hopeful despite their circumstances.

Finally, in section 5 we'll share three important topics for further thinking given the increasing cultural diversity in the United States and around the world. We've included this section because effective leadership today and into the twenty-second century requires a deeper understanding of gender, racial, economic, and lifestyle diversity than ever before. No longer will broad generalizations about people different from ourselves suffice. The United States and the world is already (not becoming) diverse in lifestyle and culture. As of 2017, "Forty-seven states and 90 percent of the counties have an absolute decline in white population under age 20. All net growth of children in this country is coming from racial and ethnic minorities."[11] Additionally, with the broad access to the Internet and cell phones, individuals increasingly expect products, services, and experiences to immediately meet their needs and make their lives better. When an experience does not deliver upon these expectations, people (yes, consumers) will explore other options. Gone are the days of limited choices and settling for what's available.

As a result, spiritual leaders must connect the stated and un-stated needs and desires of individual people and tribes to the "real presence of Christ... if they are to become conduits of Grace."[12] In his book, *Spiritual Leadership: Why Leaders Lead and Who Seekers Seek to Follow*, Tom Bandy names eight existential anxieties that are addressed by eight experiences of Christ led by eight types of spiritual leaders with different experiences and expectations. Within each of these categories there are many nuisances based on culture. No longer is there a monolithic identity of people by age, ethnicity, wealth, education, geography, or family status. Customized experiences are no longer an exception; they are an expectation, even in the church.

A recent global report cites, "Cultural diversity has emerged as a key concern at the turn of a new century. Yet the meanings attached to this catch-all term are as varied as they are shifting."[13] Some see cultural diversity within a church and community as a positive, enabling deeper understanding, relationships, and im-pact. For others, cultural differences are misunderstood, feared, and cause many conflicts. This second diagnosis is too often the reality within some churches. So, an essential challenge for leaders is to lead the way and to propose a vision of cultural diversity and thereby to clarify how, rather than being a threat to the status quo, differences in gender, race, economics and lifestyle are strengths to the church and world.

Discipleship is also a hot topic of conversation among the Christian church leaders that we support as pastors, strategists and coaches. We get lots of questions along the lines of "What's the best discipleship pathway?" or "How do we get our young people and visitors to stay?" This is an exciting question because pastors and church leaders are realizing that it takes more than weekend worship experiences to transform individual lives and the world. We are acknowledging that engagement through relationship is the real work of discipleship. Building relationship requires gathering, listening, building trust, and sharing stories. And it requires struggling with issues of faith, family, and fears. When this happens in the context of a congregation, authentic faith communities can form. Without diversity and discipleship the church is ultimately irrelevant. It will not fulfill its higher purpose of love, community and transformation. Sure the church does good deeds such as feed the hungry, comfort the broken-hearted, and advocate for justice. Yet, if these don't lead to individual or societal transformation we are not serving our higher missional purpose.

So why does this really matter?

People need more than the Sunday morning hour to experience life transformation. As a result of reading this book, gaining deeper understanding, building new relationships, and committing to new practices, we envision congregations and organizations that are more impactful across generations in discipleship and in transforming the world. We envision one-on-one conversations, small group discussions, and large gatherings initiated in homes, coffee shops, and other community spaces as often as they are shared inside the walls of a sanctuary. We imagine music as diverse as classic hymns, Christian rap, and contemporary Christian sung in multiple languages and tempos embracing the diverse nature of the people we desire to reach.

We envision a primary focus of the church on changing lives and communities instead of filling pews or rosters. This call embodies love, support, and acceptance of all people, especially at their points of need. Each day thousands of people in the communities we serve need help with housing, transportation, food, education, health care, and more. Unfortunately, the church turns many people away offering little or no help. Yet, imagine the very identity of the church once again becoming a place of empathy that connects people to resources while meeting immediate physical and deep spiritual needs. It becomes a place where people find belonging and empowerment. What an exciting journey!

Whew, take a breath...

As authors, we (Rodney, Lia, and Jasmine) represent three generations of pastors, preachers, and leaders who decided to drop our assumptions at the church doors and welcome a blank slate from which to create a renewed faith movement and to transform the world. As we go forward in this book's journey together our faith and ministry stories will be woven throughout so you'll get a sense of who we are. Our hope is that we become more than reader and author, but friends along this journey.

So with this background, let's jump in!

Section 1

THE OLD RULES

Life's most persistent and urgent question is, "What are you doing for others?"

— *Rev. Dr. Martin Luther King Jr.*

Chapter 1

OLD RULES OF THE TRADITIONALISTS (BORN 1945 OR BEFORE)

Rule 1: Follow the Rules
Rule 2: Respect the Past
Rule 3: Maintain Loyalty
Rule 4: Work Hard

Historical Context

If Rev. Dr. Martin Luther King Jr. were still alive he'd be ninety years old in 2019. We imagine he would be a patriarch of Ebenezer Baptist Church in Atlanta where he grew up. He'd be a lifetime member of the NAACP, and still be a drum major for justice. Though his deep voice would be dulled by age, his spirit would be strong as ever. Dr. King, like many of his generation, followed in the footsteps of his father and grandfather who were pastors. He followed this vocational path out of respect and loyalty, but also out of a calling. King wrote, "Of course I was religious. I grew up in the church. My father is a preacher, my grandfather was a preacher, my great-grandfather was a preacher, my only brother is a preacher, my daddy's brother is a preacher. So I didn't have much choice."[1]

Like Dr. King, the Traditionalist generation (born in 1945 or before) grew up during the 1940s, '50s and '60s and are now in their seventies, eighties, and nineties. They lived through the Great Depression, World War II, and the Vietnam War. And, it was this generation of courageous people who birthed the American civil rights movement as young adults.

Dr. King wrote in his journal: "I was born in the late twenties on the verge of the Great Depression, which was to spread its disastrous arms into every corner of this nation for over a decade. I was much too young to remember the beginning of this depression, but I do recall, when I was about five years of age, how I questioned my parents about the numerous people standing in breadlines. I can see the effects of this early childhood experience on my present anti-capitalistic feelings."[2] Like King, the people of this generation knew firsthand what it meant to be without food and to work hard for their very survival.

The United States entered World War II in 1941 and actively fought with allies until the war ended in 1945. Many who served in or lived through World War II have been forever impacted by fear, pride, and a sense of duty that comes from sacrificing for the common good. The values of loyalty, sacrifice, and pride of country are forever etched within the minds and hearts of many of this generation. Notably, Americans of all races made a significant contribution to the World War II despite the fact that the armed forces were segregated based on race. As documented in the National World War II Museum, "In 1941, fewer than 4,000 African Americans were serving in the military and only twelve African Americans had become officers. By 1945, more than 1.2 million African Americans would be serving in uniform on the Home Front, in Europe, and the Pacific (including thousands of

African American women in the Women's auxiliaries)."[3] African Americans who enlisted in the armed forces, often saw their service in the military as a road out of poverty and a path toward improved skills and greater opportunity after the war.

President Truman's Committee on Equality of Treatment and Opportunity in the Armed Services was established by Executive Order 9981, on July 26, 1948, to recommend revisions in military regulations in order to implement the government's policy of desegregation of the armed services. This meant that there was to be equality of treatment and opportunity for all members of the armed forces, regardless of race, color, religion, or national origin.[4]

While women of the Traditionalist generation often stayed home to care for children or aging parents, this trend shifted significantly during World War II when many women went to work. Some historians argue that World War II was the beginning of the modern women's rights movement. Before the war, 12 million women worked outside the home. During the war, 18 million women, or half of the women in the United States, worked outside the home. This number doesn't account for women working longer hours on farms or women of color whose number are likely unaccounted for.

The baby boom of the late 1940s and '50s represented a prosperous time in post-war America. Yet, not all Americans benefited from the booming economy, housing market, and educational opportunities. In particular, after World War II ended, many African Americans, Latinos, and Native Americans were either jobless or only able to work in low-skill positions without room for advancement, such as janitors, dishwashers, or domestics often making only a fraction of what their white counterparts would make, despite their skill level.

The immediate hopes for peace, prosperity, and equality for women and people of color were often unrealized in post-war segregated America. One woman from York, Nebraska, recalled this story of a black veteran after the war. "The war broke up a lot of prejudice," she says. "You were there to do a job. And if you can do it, you're going to do it no matter what color you are. You work next to the next guy. Your life depended on him regardless of what color they are."[5] Yet, after the war the segregation between races and classes persisted.

In 1960, King was thirty-one years old and he, like many young Americans, decided that the world in America needed to change. Racial equality was a right of every person and justice must be demanded. King along with young Americans, black and white, committed their lives to eliminate the racial injustices and culture of war that stubbornly persisted.

Half a million American soldiers served in the Vietnam War beginning in 1960, and after several years of war many began to speak out against the war. Young people in particular began to advocate for a society free of war and filled with more love. The Beatles, Elvis Presley, Marvin Gaye, Tina Turner, and Aretha Franklin were among the artists that created the sound track for an era of experimentation and freedom.

For the Traditionalist generation, the 1940s, '50s and '60s were decades where the entire culture of America shifted. They were decades of social upheaval, war, rebellion, and fear by some. Presidents Truman, Eisenhower, Kennedy, and Johnson led the nation forward.

The Religious Context

So what about the church of the 1940s, '50s, and '60s?

Many denominational churches, including The United Methodist church, grew through the 1940s and '50s, yet they began to change dramatically in the 1960s. The Methodist Church had a membership of 10,331,574 in 1965, an increase of about 27,000 since 1964. Then it lost 21,000 reported members in 1966, a trend that never reversed and continued after the 1968 merger with the Evangelical United Brethren Church.[6] Methodism had been America's largest Protestant denomination until surpassed by the Southern Baptist Convention in 1967, whose membership was more than 11 million.

During the 1940s, '50s, and '60s churches collaborated to found institutions including hospitals, social service organizations, and civic organizations such as the Boy Scouts, Girl Scouts, and the YMCA. Churches intentionally marketed their facilities for community usage led by its lay members. Importantly, lay leadership positions served as an important source of social capital in individual neighborhoods and beyond. Lay leaders used their skills and social network to gain influence within other civic organizations and in local and national politics. Despite the important positive impact of the church during these decades, critics fault the church for its "accommodation to and participation in the institution of slavery up until the Civil War . . . and in some quarters even staunch defense of—segregation in the American South."[7] However, they were guided by the rules of the time.

Beyond any single denomination, Christian America's story during these decades was in part symbolized by three iconic structures: the United Methodist Building in Washington, DC; the Interchurch Center on New York City's Upper West Side; and the Crystal Cathedral in Garden Grove, California. As author Robert P. Jones describes, "These buildings, edifices of the white Protestant Christian hope and power that rose and receded over the course of the twentieth century, represent—respectively—the high-water mark of the first wave of white mainline Protestant denominational optimism in the Roaring Twenties, the second wave of white mainline Protestant ecumenism at midcentury…"[8] Each building's massiveness and grandeur were designed to speak without words of the importance of the Protestant faith. Yet, today each of these buildings have a different purpose from their founders' ambitions. As culture has shifted each building usage has been adapted—or even been transformed in its uses. Indeed, through the declining prominence of these buildings, we can see the decline of white Protestant dominance amid the steady shift of the American religious landscape.[9]

The church of the Traditionalists was guided by the Old Rules of the Traditionalists (born in 1945 or before). When it came to faithfulness in religion and society, the rules can be summed up as:

- Follow the Rules
- Respect the Past
- Maintain Loyalty
- Work Hard

The iconic edifices, the social landscape, the religious landscape, and the church leadership positions as a source of social capital in community—while manifested in vastly different ways across race and social location—can all be attributed to the Old Rules of Traditionalists. For a time, it worked. But then, the rules changed.

Questions for Reflection

1. How have the history and traditions of your church been shaped by the Traditionalist generation? What lessons can we glean from their experience for the church today?

2. Where have you experienced the expectations to Follow the Rules, Respect the Past, Maintain Loyalty, and Work Hard?

3. In what ways are life and church different today in your community than during the 1940s and '50s?

Chapter 2

OLD RULES
OF THE BOOMERS
(BORN 1946–1964)

Rule 1: Break the Rules

Rule 2: Education

Rule 3: Do Justice

Historical Context

The year 2019 marks an important landmark in American culture as the youngest Boomers turn fifty-five and the oldest turn seventy-three. This generation born between 1946 and 1964 makes up nearly 20 percent of the US population and has significantly shifted US culture. Baby Boomers, as a generation, grew up in the 1950s and 1960s.[1] They are called Boomers because of the boom of babies born after World War II. Some of the most famous items found in the home of Boomers as they grew up in America were likely the dial-up phone, Tang juice drink, and diverse music from the Beetles to Jimmy Hendrix to Diana Ross and the Supremes. And, many believe the August 2018 death of Aretha Franklin marks the end of an era for Boomers.

Some of most defining moments of the 1960s in the United States include the Vietnam War, the assassination of President

Kennedy, the Civil Rights Movement and assassination of leaders Dr. Martin Luther King, Jr. and Malcom X. After World War II the American economy grew and supported larger families and advances in technology such as instant cameras, television remote controls, and audio tape recorders. But the Boomers' era was also marked by great unrest. Americans born during this period were shaped by a nation divided by the Vietnam War and the fight for justice and equity for women and people of color in the United States.

The civil rights movement was instrumental to the 1960s because it enabled legislative change for racial and gender equity that would impact future generations. The Civil Rights Act of 1964 eliminated segregation and enabled integration in public restaurants, theaters, hotels, retail stores, employment, schools, hospitals, swimming pools, libraries, and other public spaces. "This act, signed into law by President Lyndon Johnson on July 2, 1964, prohibited discrimination in public places, provided for the integration of schools and other public facilities, and made employment discrimination illegal. This document was the most sweeping civil rights legislation since Reconstruction."[2]

A vivid piece of the history of this generation is also found in the 1973 celebration of International Women's Day, in speeches by Equal Rights Amendment supporters and in a 1970s rally by women fighting to gain child care support.[3] This is the era where the personal became overtly political through activism. Gay and lesbian activists demanded equal rights and celebrated their identities. 1969 was especially significant, as the Stonewall uprising in New York City propelled activists around the United States into action leading to annual pride parades celebrating freedom of gender and sexuality.[4]

Today I (Lia) had the opportunity to coach a Boomer female pastor. She is a capable leader who is serving as pastor of two congregations. One old and one new. One congregation is filled with a rich history, but steadily declining due to illness and death of aging members. The other congregation is a recovery church that's growing with mostly young twenty- and thirty-year-old Millennials who are seeking recovery from drugs, alcohol, incarceration, and abuse. This Boomer pastor is caught between two generations and faithfully trying to bridge the gap.

One of the most recognizable Boomers of today is Oprah Winfrey. She was born on an isolated farm in Kosciusko, Mississippi, on January 29, 1954. Her name was supposed to be Orpah, from the Bible, but because of the difficulty of spelling and pronunciation, she was known as Oprah almost from birth.[5] Baby Boomers like Oprah obtained a higher level of education than any generation before them. About 88 percent of Boomers completed high school, and 28 percent obtained a bachelor's degree or higher. Oprah's college career was fueled by a full scholarship to Tennessee State University after winning a public speaking contest.[6] Over the course of her career as a reporter, producer, host, global media leader, and philanthropist, Oprah Winfrey has created an unparalleled connection with people around the world; she has entertained, enlightened, and uplifted millions of viewers for thirty years. She is one of the most influential and admired public figures in the world today, and some regard her *Super Soul Sunday* program as their "church." She promotes living spiritually, mindfully, and consciously. Oprah, like many people, loves gospel music, food, conversations, and "aha" moments.

Religious Context

When Pope John XXIII opened the Second Vatican Council (also known as Vatican II) on October 11, 1962, in Rome at the Vatican it was a historic moment for the world. There hadn't been an assembly of Roman Catholic religious leaders to address church doctrine in nearly 100 years. Over two thousand Roman Catholic bishops from around the world and thousands of observers, auditors, media, sisters, laymen, and laywomen attended the council between 1962 and 1965. The purpose of this assembly was to give new direction for the life of the Catholic Church after World War II. Sixteen documents in total came out of the Council, laying a foundation for the Catholic Church and ecumenical relationships as we know it today. The Vatican II documents allowed clergy relationships to be more collegial, freedom of worship across languages to encourage greater participation by laity, and cultural adaptations. Importantly, lay ministries of the Catholic Church were established including participation in worship and affirming that every Christian by virtue of baptism has gifts and talents to share through ministries of service. Vatican II also endorsed good relationships across Christian denominations including allowing Catholics to participate in Protestant weddings and prayer across religions. This also includes respect and love for the Jews and a renouncement of anti-Semitism. Additionally, the Council affirmed that every person has human dignity and is created in the image of God. As a result, it encouraged governments to support the freedom of religious liberty and separation of church and state. Finally, Vatican II supported an openness to non-Christian religions.[7] While this one document was neither flawless nor unanimous in its church teaching or practice, this was a significant reform, updating and changing the Catholic Church and impacting the global Protestant church as well.[8]

(Rev. Dr. Rodney T. Smothers) I am a Baby Boomer. My generational identity has shaped so much of my attitude toward church and toward life. I grew up in a family where my mother was Baptist, my father, Church of God. They never left their respective churches. So I was Baptamethocostal. I never shook that. That stayed with me most of my life. I never really joined either of these churches although I was very involved. My mother was an usher in her church for over fifty years. My dad served as a minister in his church.

So we stayed involved in church and then when I was a young adult I become apart of A. P. Shaw Church in Southeast Washington. That was where I was really led into a meaningful relationship with Jesus Christ. A. P. Shaw was known as the Holy Ghost headquarters. It was a vibrant United Methodist Church. It had several choirs, many ministries, and a culture of evangelistic outreach that was second to none. The irony was that my pastor was a licensed local pastor who served that church for over thirty years and it grew, grew, grew and it's in that vibrant spiritual environment that I came to Christ. This early experience in diverse church backgrounds has provided me with an appreciation for the difference in church traditions. When I had the opportunity to serve as an adjunct worship professor at the Interdenominational Theological Center— Gammon Seminary, that early background provided a rich appreciation for how the church can come at worship, polity and service from different lens. Today, it appears that some younger generations of worshippers don't always have the depth of theological perspective that fueled the traditional forms of worship. This is not to say that their worship is not effective. It is that I believe that there is something to be retained in the "why" of what we do in worship. While worship or entertainment dominates the conversation about worship design, the real question is about "depth" and "substance."

Overall, the Boomer generation will experience a substantial decline in numbers in the coming decades, and the pace of decline is expected to accelerate as Boomers grow older. "When the first baby boomers turned 65 in 2011, there were just under 77 million Baby Boomers in the population. By 2030, when the baby boomers will be between 66 and 84 years old, that number is projected to drop to 60 million and decrease further by 2060 to only 2.4 million."[9] This decline, coupled with increases in immigration and births to minority populations, is projected to produce an increasingly diverse US population in the years to come.

Today, more than 50 percent of all United Methodist pastors (and many mainline denominations) are Boomers. One of the key questions today and even more into the future is, how will Boomers leave a legacy for future ministry of the church and community as ten thousand boomers retire everyday between now and 2029?[10]

(Pastor Jasmine) I serve an extremely diverse, urban congregation in which much of the leadership team are Boomers (of all races, social locations, and sexual orientations) who have come back to faith or raised their children in the church. They almost always have a "gap" in their church life during which they left the church. Theses Boomers, like my parents, love their church and community and yet, express it in vastly different ways from the other generations. We often have to "translate" to see that we are all on the same page. The Traditionalists are tired but still want their word to count; the Boomers are finally getting their voice to carry with the Traditionalists; Gen Xers are sparse; yet, the Millennials won't stay around if they aren't heard. As the Lead Pastor, (a member of the microgeneration, Xennials) I'm the translator, peacemaker and challenger. Like the songwriter says, "Can't we all just get along?"

Everyone brings their own rules to the table…and expects others to play by their rulebook. Yet, the Boomers bring a different set of rules than those of the Traditionalists. The Old Rules of the Boomers (born 1946–1964) can be summed up as:

- Break the Rules
- Education
- Do Justice

The Boomers, who have radically changed the landscape of American society and religion, are now turning their attention to the church and life legacy. However, yet again, the rules have changed.

Questions for Reflection

1. How have the history and traditions of your church been shaped by the Boomer generation?

2. What do you appreciate most about this generation? What lessons can we glean from their experience for the church today?

3. In what ways are life and church different today than during the 1960s, '70s?

Chapter 3

OLD RULES OF GENERATION XERS (BORN 1965–1980)

Rule 1: Be Skeptical

Rule 2: Rewrite the Rules

Rule 3: Accept "True for You but Not for Me"

Rule 4: Embrace Life and Family over Work

Historical Context

Rush, rush, rush…Generation X (Gen X) is the generation that experienced a hurried childhood filled with latch keys, Little League sports, and family migration from cities to suburbs. As teens and young adults Generation X feared the HIV/AIDS epidemic, witnessed urban decay, and are dubbed the "computer generation" as the proliferation of computers took hold in schools and some homes.[1] In jobs, many Gen Xers are the first generation to embrace the risks and rewards of entrepreneurship and choose to work in smaller organizations affording more life balance rather than seek big corporations, government jobs, and the perceived promise of stability and retirement accounts. From grunge to hip-hop, Gen X's diverse culture emerged uniquely and became more mainstream in time. Today, Gen Xers range from forties to mid-fifties in age.

I (Lia) am a Generation Xer, born in 1972 to Baby Boomer parents. My African American parents grew up during the civil rights movement. I was birthed out of the movement. Before migrating to St. Louis at the age of fourteen, my mother was raised in a segregated rural Mississippi community. Her family is documented in the National Civil Rights Museum in Memphis, Tennessee, for its work in Mississippi registering African Americans to vote in the 1950s and early '60s. My father grew up in St. Louis. Both attended racially segregated grade schools, but my mother attended a desegregated high school. As a college student my dad was actively involved in integrating restaurant lunch counters in Kirksville, Missouri, with the leadership of a Methodist Campus minister and the Young Democrats Club.

My parents' struggle and the sacrifices of many from the Traditionalist and Boomer generations shaped the course of my life even before I was aware of its impact. Growing up a few miles from Ferguson, Missouri, in St. Louis County, I benefited from racially integrated schools and had many options to study, shop, and eat. America progressed tremendously from the 1930s to the '80s on issues of racial inclusion in education, housing, and jobs. My generation has been the first generation to broadly benefit from the civil rights and women's rights movements. I always felt I could do anything with hard work despite being African American and a girl.

Politically, many Generation Xers today care more about practical issues than party affiliation and would rather volunteer than simply vote (or sit on boards). Gen Xers are middle-aged adults with children spanning from preschool to college who have been jaded by 9/11, wars in the Middle East, and long-term debt from student loans, mortgages, and credit cards. They are the "sandwich generation" who are caring for parents, children and grandchildren. They are resilient survivors, seeking to enjoy life and find rest from its busyness for the sake of themselves and their families. Famous American Gen Xers include Barack and Michelle Obama, Tom Cruise, and Michael Jordan.

My faith as a child was nurtured at home and in Lutheran Missouri Synod schools and church. In 1979 as a seven year old I can remember learning to pray, reading scripture, attending Friday Night Spaghetti Suppers at church (a fund raiser for the school PTA), and being baptized in church. It was the only time I sat on the front row with both of my parents at church. As a young child family, school, and sports filled our life. My brother Anthony and I took swim lessons at the local YMCA on Saturday mornings. He played little league football and I was a cheerleader in the fall. We both ran AAU track in the summers and traveled to track meets most every weekend. We had a busy life filled with love. Unlike many in our parents' Boomer Generation our social life revolved around family and sports, not the church. While my mom, brother, and I attended church on many Sundays, many our closest friends were from school or our sports teams.

According to a Pew Research Study, Gen Xers are described as the bridge generation and are

> bookended by two much larger generations—the Baby Boomers ahead and the Millennials behind—that are strikingly different from one another. And in most of the ways we take stock of generations—their racial and ethnic makeup; their political, social and religious values; their economic and educational circumstances; their technology usage—Gen Xers are a low-slung, straight-line bridge between two noisy behemoths.[2]

21

For me (Jasmine), Gen Xers are missing in the church but have vastly reshaped the landscape of business and society. The church has suffered for their absence since their youth group days. People who write articles like, "Whatever Happened to Generation X?;"[3] "Generation X—not millennials—is changing the nature of work;"[4] and "Why You Need To Pay Attention To Gen X Leaders,"[5] suggest that Gen X is missing from society as a whole. Yet, from soccer with the kids to assisted living with the parents, this anti-establishment generation is over-stretched and under-supported. They tout the deceased Nirvana rocker, Kurt Cobain, as the voice of the generation the way Boomers hold up John Lennon as their iconic voice. Nirvana brought alternative rock and grunge to the mainstream. Kurt Cobain struggled with depression, heroin addiction and reportedly, died by suicide at the age of twenty-seven. Gen Xers are my friends, cousins and colleagues. Yet, the church is neither their home nor the nucleus of life. In my experience, Gen Xers know God and have faith; they just can't add one more thing or fight in one more place. I miss my Gen X friends in church; however, I love to meet them on the way to the next thing (meeting, kid's game, parents' retirement party, concert, vacation, and so on)…and welcome and celebrate their skepticism.

Gen Xers are independent thinkers who grew up learning to be skeptical of old ways and to express their creativity. After seeing their Boomer parents experience divorce, downsizing, and disaffection in their work, Gen Xers have embraced innovation using technology and new approaches to work differently and in more productive ways. For example, Gen X working women have initiated the work from home, job sharing, entrepreneurship, and work-life balance movements that Millennials are continuing to recreate and benefit from today.

Within Generation X we see clear shifts within the United States becoming less white and more multi-racial (49 percent of Generation Xers are non-white), marrying at later ages, and being more educated than their parents. An example of these shifts is seen within parenting. Today, one in four parents living with a child in the United States are unmarried. Driven by declines in marriage overall, as well as increases in births outside of marriage, this marks a dramatic change from a half-century ago, when fewer than one in ten parents living with their children were unmarried (7 percent). Interestingly, solo mothers—those who are raising at least one child with no spouse or partner in the home—no longer dominate the ranks of unmarried parents as they once did. In 1968, 88 percent of unmarried parents fell into this category. By 1997 that share had dropped to 68 percent, and in 2017 the share of unmarried parents who were solo mothers declined to 53 percent. These declines in solo mothers have been entirely offset by increases in cohabitating parents: now 35 percent of all unmarried parents are living with a partner. Meanwhile, the share of unmarried parents who are solo fathers has held steady at 12 percent.[6] These trends began with Boomers and became mainstream with Gen X whose culture of diversity and inclusion in values, lifestyle, and religion can be described as "what's true for you doesn't have to be for me" or "live and let live."

Religious Context

So have Gen Xers become more or less religious? According to the Pew Research Center's 2014 US Religious Landscape Study, including a nationally representative telephone survey of 35,071 adults, the percentages who say they believe in God, pray daily, and regularly go to church or other religious services all declined modestly from 2007 to 2014.[7] About a quarter of US adults (27 percent overall and up to 30 percent of Gen X) now say they think of themselves as spiritual but not religious, up eight to ten percentage points in five years. This growth has been broad-based: It has occurred among men and women; whites, blacks, and Hispanics; people of many different ages and education levels; and among Republicans and Democrats. For instance, the share of whites who identify as spiritual but not religious has grown by eight percentage points from 2012 to 2017.[8]

As the US population ages and older, more religiously observant generations die out, they are being replaced by far less religious young adults. One example: two-thirds of members of the Traditionalist Generation (67 percent) say religion is very important in their lives, but only 50 percent of Generation X and 38 percent of the youngest members of the Millennial generation—those born between 1990 and 1996—say the same. Just 34 percent of Gen X and 28 percent of the youngest Millennials report attending religious services at least weekly, compared with about half (51 percent) of their Traditionalist Generation counterparts.[9]

Generation X is also reportedly one of the most skeptical generations to date, having grown up in an era when many of the institutions built by Traditionalists and Boomers were acquired, transformed, or dismantled. Gen Xers saw corporations like Enron crumble, churches like the Crystal Cathedral fail, and watched live media coverage of the devastating 9/11 terrorist attacks. So, yes, Gen Xers are skeptical. In a professional setting, this means they have a tendency to push back on ideas. Boomers can feel like

Gen Xers are disrespecting their ideas, but most Gen Xers push back and ask tough questions because they care. As a result, Gen Xers are important contributors to teams as they bridge the gap across generations.

The overwhelming number of life choices have pushed spirituality to the sidelines for many Gen Xers. Busyness and preoccupation with other activities make it difficult to place spiritual things at the center of their lives. In some ways faith in working hard and achievement make it difficult to prioritize spirituality. Yet, some churches are finding that combining practical life activities like soccer and ACT prep classes with relevant spiritual opportunitities like prayer partners and offering holy communion during the week is creating new excitement for discipleship in some peoples' lives. Combining practical life skills with relevant spiritual opportunities is creating new excitement for discipleship in peoples' lives. People are searching for deeper meaning in their lives beyond just material things.

Generation Xers have a voice that is often rebuffed in church. The Old Rules of Gen Xers lends to "side-eye" in church. People wonder, "Can we ask THOSE questions in church?" Old Rules of Generation Xers (born 1965–1980):

- Be Skeptical
- Rewrite the Rules
- Accept "True for you but not for me."
- Embrace Life and family over work

The rules have led to an absence in church for this generation. And yet, the rules are still changing. . . .

25

Questions for Reflection

1. How have the history and traditions of your church been shaped by Generation X? What lessons can we glean from their experience for the church today?

2. Where have you experienced the realities for religious diversity, skepticism, rewriting the rules, and a desire for life and family over work?

3. In what ways are life and church different today than during the 1980s and '90s?

Section 2
THE NEW RULES

So then, if anyone is in Christ, that person is part of the new creation. The old things have gone away, and look, the new things have arrived!

—2 Corinthians 5:17 (CEB)

Chapter 4

NEW RULES OF MILLENNIALS (BORN 1981–1995)

Rule 1: Be Connected and Mobile

Rule 2: Always Have a Side Gig That's Creative

Rule 3: Find a Community, Not an Institution

Rule 4: Be Authentic, Inclusive, and Rebellious

Millennials (those born in the early 1980s through the late 1990s) live a life that appears contradictory to some members of other generations. As young adults in their twenties and thirties, Millennials are tech savvy, socially-conscious, and ambitious; yet, they are often perceived by older generations as lazy and self-centered. Older Millennials are passionate and committed to their career or work. They are not afraid to switch jobs or professions as they experiment with and explore how to live out their passions through meaningful work. Yet, careers and work are not what is most central to the identity of Millennials. In a Barna survey of over five hundred Millennials, "Family" and "personal interests" are the top two categories. "Career" is actually one of the least likely categories to be named as central to the identity of Millennials—the only category it beats is "technology."[1]

Rule 1: Be Connected and Mobile.

Millennials are the first generation for whom a "phone" has been primarily a video game, direction finder, and research library all at once.[2] Millennials are digital natives and have never known a world without laptops and iPhones. When talking to Millennials at a recent conference, one Millennial said, "I'm going to be on my phone all the time looking things up. It's just the way it is." Whether in church or hanging out with friends, Millennials are hyperconnected with friends on social media, researching topics of interest, and checking out the latest YouTube videos. Because of technology, Millennials are also the mobile generation who can comfortably work from anywhere on their phones, tablets, or laptops. They love the freedom to travel, work, and integrate fun. In fact, many Millennials say they're always working because they're always connected and responsive.

I (Lia) am the aunt of a millennial nephew who was born in 1994. At the age of twenty-three he's a new college graduate, and like many Millennials he is tech savvy and hyperconnected to his friends via social media. He posts on Instagram, Facebook, and Snapchat throughout the day on topics spanning his social activities, sports, world events, and job inquiries. He finds community most easily online and does not hesitate to "keep it real" by authentically sharing his opinions online. As a Gen X aunt, I may not always agree with his points of view, but I do respect his freedom to express personal values.

For Millennials, globalization—whether traveling internationally, buying products online from retailers outside the US, or connecting with foreign friends via social media—has always been a fact of life. Millennials have also been called the "instant" generation. This is not because they have ever experienced Folgers instant coffee, but because they cannot remember a time when they had to wait for anything. Think about instant messaging, Amazon same-day delivery, and online gaming with friends in real time. And thankfully Millennials have always had Emojis to cheer them up!

Rule 2: Always Have a Side Gig That's Creative to Challenge Me!

Millennials who have grown up in a capitalistic western society often think of themselves as consumers and entrepreneurs. Some of the parents of Millennials have paid a lot of money for teachers to teach them and sports coaches to train them. For others, as students they are incurring thousands of dollars in student loan debt. On average 53 percent of students ages eighteen to twenty-nine are incurring debt to pay for educational expenses. As of 2017, the median level of student loan debt for all adults was $17,000 and the average for Millennials was $32,731.[3] As a result, Millennials' view of money or stewardship is mixed. They believe in the dreams of financial freedom, but few see an easy pathway toward the lifestyle they desire, even with college degrees. YouTube vloggers, young professional athletes, and reality TV stars are the new celebrities who make millions of dollars endorsing products online with seemingly little effort. Yet, many Millennials are disappointed when they can't reproduce these results. Still, a Millennial recently said, "We're the hustling generation. We are strong willed, passionate, and trail blazers. We're finding many ways to make income and make a difference."[4]

Inside the church we spend much of our time managing what we have control over and not enough time immersed in what we do not understand. We talk about Millennials, yet spend very little time with people who are in their twenties and thirties and who are different from us. As I (Lia) had lunch recently with a UMC District Superintendent she commented that we do not have one African American or Hispanic Pastor in over 100 churches in her district. What an eye-opening moment. If the demographics of her district were 100 percent Anglo then nothing would be wrong. Yet, the district is diverse racially, and the congregations do not reflect this diversity. If we are to be a church for diverse Millennials and younger generations then nurturing diverse leadership is essential. In fact, it's an authentic way of life for many Millennials.

Millennials have also grown up in a freelance or "gig" economy. A recent Fast Company Article stated, "Across the U.S., there are approximately 53 million freelancers—people who work on a contract basis for multiple entities, rather than being employed by a single company. They make up around 36% of the total workforce, and collectively, they contribute around $1.4 trillion to the U.S. economy. If current trends hold steady, by 2027 the majority of Americans will be freelancers, according to a study commissioned by the freelance marketplace Upwork."[5] In order to make sense of these statistics, it's important to recognize that Millennials are struggling to find jobs even if they have college degrees. The employment rate of Millennials in 2017, an analysis of unemployment numbers for the month of December 2017 released by the Bureau of Labor Statistics (BLS), revealed that 4.1 of US adults ages sixteen and older are unemployed (6.6

million people). Yet, 7.1 percent of twenty- to twenty-five-year-olds are unemployed. Even young adults with bachelor's degrees are struggling to find jobs. So, for Millennials, getting a job and starting a career often happens later and includes time to explore options beyond the traditional career ladder during their twenties and thirties out of choice or necessity.[6]

Rule 3: Find a Community, Not an Institution.

Millennials want to belong to a group of people where they can know one another and be known. Communities of belonging (not obligation) is what they desire. Millennials want to be inspired and feel they "get to" be apart of something that's changing the world instead of "got to." Some Millennials grew up going to church because it was expected by their parents or grandparents. They were taught to be a good person and to serve the community. Yet as adults, once Millennials have a choice, many are choosing to explore spiritually and serve in ways that are nontraditional from the view point of their Generation X or Boomer parents and grandparents. Millennials are the least churched adult generation and the least likely either to identify as Christian or to say faith is very important to their life.[7]

Related to religion, many Millennials, even those who have grown up in the church, have ambivalent relationship with the church. One Millennial said, "From the depths of my heart, I want to love church. I want to be head-over-heels for church like the unshakeable Ned Flanders (from The Simpsons). I want to send global, sky-writing airplanes telling the life-change that happens beneath a steeple. I want to install a police microphone on top of my car, and cruise the streets screaming to the masses about the magical utopian community of believers waiting for them just down the street. I desperately want to feel this way about church, but I don't. Not even a little bit. In fact, like much of my generation, I feel the complete opposite. Turns out I identify more with Maria from the Sound of Music, staring out of the abbey window, longing to be free."[8]

Lia is right! Being a Millennial in church is tantamount to being Scotty Smalls in the 1993 movie, *The Sandlot*. (Yes, I know the movie was set in 1962 but stay with me, ok?) You're the new kid on the block; you're growing up; you desperately want to be a part of the community; but everyone wonders if you can fit in...on their terms. And most importantly, you don't know how (and really don't want) to play baseball by their rules! Your identity is expressed through the new rules of engagement: be connected and be mobile; always have a side gig that's creative; find a community, not an institution; be authentic, inclusive, and rebellious. Man, are we out of place! And our Gen X cousins, whom we've relied on for guidance and translation, aren't around to help us out! And all of a sudden, everyone is depending on us to save an institution that we're not connected to and clean up a mess that we didn't create. The church spends much of its time fighting about things that don't matter to me or that my generation has already figured out. Human sexuality; racism; sexism; ageism; classism; xenophobia—we've been in classrooms with all different kinds of people since pre-school! While we hold different beliefs, many of us don't understand why the church is so late to the ministry of inclusion—it feels like a Jesus mandate to us! Sometimes, I (Jasmine) just want to tell the church, "You're killing me, Smalls!"

Fifty-five million adults, eight million of which are twenty-somethings, have left the church, and it seems like everyone is trying to figure out why.[9] Although the answers vary from person to person, there are some general trends that apply across generations that impact this striking trend of religious "nones."

According to the 2014 Pew Research Religious Landscape Study Religious "nones,'—people who self-identify as atheists or agnostics, as well as those who say their religion is "nothing in particular"—now make up roughly 23 percent of the US adult population. This is a profound increase from 2007, the last time a similar Pew Research study was conducted, when 16 percent of Americans were "nones." (During this same time period, those who self identify as Christians have fallen from 78 percent to 71 percent.)[10] Importantly, the vast majority of the religious "nones" (78 percent) say they were raised as Christians or members of another faith but that they now have no religious affiliation.[11] And, if the church doesn't respond this trend will continue. This is an important statement, so it's worth repeating. It's the church's responsibility to respond to cultural shifts. The church cannot blame individuals for leaving or never engaging with the church. Blame will only serve to accelerate the decline.

Rule 4: Be Authentic, Inclusive, and Rebellious in a Positive Way.

A Millennial United Methodist pastor, born in 1983, joined me for a recent coaching call. He is Mexican by birth and American by choice. He is a "Dreamer," an immigrant who arrived in the United States as a fifteen-year-old, but who isn't a permanent US citizen. He attended high school and college in

Iowa and seminary in Missouri. At the time of this writing, he is the Senior Pastor of a small congregation in rural Missouri, a community organizer, and Latin dance instructor. He is a devoted husband, passionate preacher, caring pastor, and a prophetic voice in his community. As a "Dreamer" he is watching and waiting for Congress to act on immigration legislation and wrote this recent Facebook post on his personal profile:

> In regards to the DREAM Act, people always ask about the law, protecting the constitution and the Bible. Here are my two cents: I am a DACA recipient and I am not breaking any laws. They did a background check on me when I applied for DACA. If I had a criminal record, I wouldn't have been able to obtain DACA. Currently, it is almost impossible to come to the U.S. with documents for countries that are non white such as Latin America countries. In regards to the law, it used to be legal to own slaves, women couldn't vote, segregation used to be legal in the U.S. Someone had to break and change those laws. Immigration reform is Biblical. Deuteronomy 23:3 denies citizenship to Moabites into Israel yet a couple books later you find Ruth the Moabite coming to Israel and being used by God. Ephesians 2:19 grants citizenship to everyone. Just because something is a law today doesn't mean that is morally right. Since our laws and our constitution were written by wealthy white men, they have been changed and amended from the moment they had been written in order to make them more just. Today, DREAMERS simply ask for the DREAM Act to pass. The DREAM Act will give us the option to apply and get citizenship.

This as an example of what it's like for some Millennials in America today navigating the challenges of diversity, identity, belonging, career, faith, and more. Their message to the world is to be authentic, inclusive, and sometimes rebellious in a positive way. This ordained pastor has continued to pursue his vocational calling as part of The United Methodist Church and was ordained an elder in full connection in June 2018.

As the father of Jasmine, Jason, and Laken, I can tell you that the conversations are interesting when we all get together. Jasmine is actually a Xennial (bridge between Gen X and Millennial). Jason and Lakeno are both Millennials but on opposite spectrums. Jason is at the beginning of the generational spectrum, and Laken is what some call post millennial—on the cusp of the Generation Y and Z. Coming from a more cautious generation, my children are much freer in their thoughts and dreams than I am. They are not bound by the restrictions of my generation and tend to think that they are free to do anything their hearts desire. While I tend to count the cost, in many ways they are more faith filled than I am when pursuing their goals without that inner voice cautioning them to go slow and conserve for a rainy day. The societal boundaries around race, sexuality, and culture do not confine them to old traditions and standards. They are more prone to take risks because they are in generations without limits. Their boldness is faith personified. They strive for the undiscovered and know that if they don't meet their goal another opportunity will come along.

Another group of Millennials recently said it this way, "We want to live the scripture, not just hear about the word of God. We want to feed the hungry and hit the streets to protest to change the world. We are already living the way forward by being inclusive. We are friends with all kinds of people accepting humanity in all its forms. Make the world a better place if you're going to invest your time."[12]

I (Jasmine) am a Millennial—well, really I'm a part of a micro-generation (a generation within a generation) called Xennials.[13] We're a hybrid of Gen Xers and Millennials born in the late 1970s to early '80s. Remember the computer game Oregon Trail? Yep, that's my generation. We played Oregon Trail at school and at home almost every day! Currently, I serve as lead pastor for the historic Atlanta First United Methodist Church. I am their first female, first African American, and youngest lead pastor in its history. I recently wrote an article for the Lewis Center for Church Leadership focused on cross cultural-racial leadership that also applies to cross generational ministry. It's reprinted here with permission from the Lewis Center:[14]

> Unique challenges arise when a church is served by a pastor from a different racial or cultural background or as it struggles to engage a changing community. Congregations and pastors often struggle in cross-cultural ministry settings for the simple reason that people fear what they do not know. While change and transformation are at the heart of the gospel, they can be very difficult for human beings. So, it's important to talk about and live change in such a way that it is transformational rather than scary or something to be avoided.

Cross-cultural ministry is deeply contextual. It's an ongoing process of figuring it out as you go along.

Focusing on Mission and Vision

One way to prepare a congregation for cross-cultural ministry is to focus intentionally on mission and vision. Why do we exist as a church? Why do we do what we do? What are the practical and tangible ways we are called to be disciples and to make disciples in our current context? We need to be clear about why we open the doors of the church every day if people are to move beyond their comfort zones and become relevant and engaged in their community again.

Acknowledging the Need for Change

It takes extraordinary spiritual maturity for people to change something they don't see as broken. It's often stress or tragedy that cause us to sit up and pay attention to the need for change—when worship attendance gets low, when money gets tight, when you begin to doubt that your congregation's legacy can survive. At First Atlanta, the congregation affirmatively decided that it didn't want to die. But an openness to change can also come through systematic preaching, learning, planning, and implementing. There are people in every church who really do believe and follow the mandates of Christ to love our neighbors and who will call the church to account for not doing so.

Worship

One challenge in a cross-cultural ministry setting is getting people to buy into a variety of worship styles and music. At First Atlanta, we sing hymns in a lot of different ways—we do really high church and really fun, flexible, post-modern church. Regardless of the style, we strive for excellence because, if you do it really well, then people simply can't complain about it. When people see that diverse types of music and worship are leading people to the heart of Jesus, they'll understand why it's important, even if they don't like it.

A smaller congregation with fewer resources to support excellence in worship and music might seek to interact with a local school. Schools have a pulse on what's relevant to the community, so a strong partnership with the school's music or drama department can strengthen the church's worship and music. You need to be willing to try and evaluate new ideas. You need to be humble enough to acknowledge that some of the best approaches may come from beyond your congregation. It's important to get outside the walls, build relationships, and learn some new skills.

Keep Things in Perspective

Pastors serving in cross-racial settings need to understand that not every issue or problem is about race. They need safe spaces to let go of frustrations and regain perspective and some really good friends who can objectively say, "I don't think that's really about you." It helps to grow a thick skin and stay deeply reflective and prayerful.

Cross-cultural ministry is deeply contextual. So, it's important to not try to replicate what someone else is doing, but rather discover what works in your setting. It's an ongoing process of figuring it out as you go along. But sharing ideas, stories, and resources can provide help and inspiration.

Questions for Reflection

1. What do you appreciate most about the Millennial Generation? What lessons can we glean from its experience for the church today?

2. How are the leadership, theology, and practice of ministry of your church being shaped by Millennials?

3. What shifts could you make in leadership, theology, and practice of ministry to better connect with Millennials? What will it take to create a "blank slate" with those in your congregation who, purposefully or accidentally, silence Millennials? What will we need to teach? What will you need to learn?

4. What will it take to create a "blank slate" with Millennials in your community who have pre-existing connotations and assumptions of "church"? What will you need to learn? What will you need to share?

NEW RULES
OF GENERATION Z
(BORN 1996–2010)

Rule 1: Give Me the WiFi Password Please

Rule 2: Don't Make Me Separate

Rule 3: Make a Difference

Rule 4: Accept That I May Be Spiritual but Not Religious

Generation Z or Gen Z are the young adults and teens born after the Millennials from 1996–2010. This generation, who grew up in the late 1990s and early 2000s, is also sometimes called the I Generation, I Gen, or post-Millennials. This generation also represents significant cultural shifts that began with Millennials but are now more pronounced with youth and young adults ages nine to twenty-three.

Four New Rules of Generation Z

Rule 1: Give me the WiFi password please. "What's the WiFi password?" I (Lia) am the parent of two Gen Z children born in 2006 and 2008 respectively. They have never known a world without WiFi and a device to connect with from tablets to phones to laptops. They got their first cell phones at the ages of eight and six years old respectively (similar to some of their latch-key friends who let themselves in the house after school and need to check in with parents). Because the Internet was commercialized in 1995, Generation Z doesn't know a world without Internet and WiFi. They have always been immersed in a world where smart phones are the norm; videos are mobile; and twenty-four-hour, instant access to people and ideas are expected. Gen Z is online everyday, often every hour. While Internet access has accelerated the availability of information for Generation Z (Alexa, Siri, or Google can answer most questions quickly), there's also the risk of information overload with little conversation or interaction with others for this generation. What is unique for Gen Z is that all of the above have been part of their lives from the start.[1] The iPhone launched in 2007 when the oldest Gen Zers were about eight years old. YouTube, Instagram, Snapchat, constant connectivity, on-demand TV, and on-demand communication are innovations Gen Z can't imagine living without because they never have.

As a result of the proliferation of technology, remote work is an expectation for Generation Z. They believe, "If I can log-on and log-in I'm at school or work." Generation Z benefited from seeing parents who have modeled working from home so it's normal for them to expect that work doesn't revolve around an office or desk. Additionally, many have taken online classes in high school or college with limited need to meet face-to-face to get good grades or even complete group projects. They are comfortable meeting using Google Hangout, FaceTime, Zoom, GoTo Meeting, or the many new technology platforms that are developing.

For our twelve- and ten-year-old sons, one of their favorite pastimes is playing video games. In fact there's a new obsession with the latest games as they debut every year around the holidays. What's unique about this digital native generation is that they've never known a world without video games that are remotely played with others in real time. This is a form of community where players talk with one another via headsets and chat using keyboards and controllers from all over the world. There is no longer any separation of time and space when there's always a friend online to play with. There's no waiting for a particular time to start or person to arrive. Gamers are connected by their passion of the game, not time, place, or personality. This same principle applies for social media where their instant stories are created, feelings shared, and newsfeeds updated each second. Additionally, Generation Z often believes the opinion of their peers online when looking for products and services more than traditional advertising.

Rule 2: Don't make me separate. For this generation there's little separation between work and life as both happen simultaneously, seven days a week. Generation Z, unlike some Millennials, are very realistic and believe they need to work hard to succeed. This belief often comes from growing up in a world that's uncertain and constantly changing. As a result, as children they learned to creatively blend school and sports, homework, and video games. As young adults they now blend work and recreation, travel and business, social media and client meetings for example. As a result, while outsiders may perceive these young adults as lacking commitment at times, the reality is that Generation Z blends the two, wants clear goals, and will work hard to deliver upon expectations. Their coping process has resulted in a strong sense of independence and an entrepreneurial spirit. According to a study by Northeastern University, a "notable 42 percent of Generation Z respondents expect to work for themselves during their careers."[2] But their goal is not simply economic security. They are marked by a very strong sense of wanting to make a difference—and believing that they can and will.

Rule 3: Help me make a difference. One of the most pronounced rules that began with Millennials and now expands with Gen Z is a desire to have unique experiences, pursue diverse careers, and make the world better. This rule is demonstrated by Project Change The World. It is a mega-movement revolving around the belief that we can all make a difference. Every act of love and kindness, no matter how big or small, matters. Sometimes, even the simplest of things, such as holding the door open for a stranger or smiling more, can have the biggest of impacts. So whether a person donates money regularly to a charity, helps an elderly person cross the street, or participates in a religious organization he or she is part of this movement that believes it's absolutely necessary to make a difference in a world full of needs. Generation Z won't tell you specifically how to make a positive change but each person inspires one another. The important thing is that you activate your own faith and gifts to shine light into the darkness. "Whether you enjoy working with children, helping animals, or cleaning up the earth, we're all in this together. As a result, we must come together with one unbreakable purpose: 'To carry one another, rather than destroy each other.'"[3]

Rule 4: Accept that I may be spiritual but not religious. Importantly, for a religious context, the most defining characteristic of Generation Z is that it is the first generation in the United States that will have been raised in a context that is post-Christian with a worldview without the Christian faith at its center. They've never known a time when sports weren't played on Sunday mornings, shopping wasn't 24/7, or there was an expectation that everyone went to church. "As a result, it is the first post-Christian generation. Yes, most people of Generation Z still believe in the existence of God (78 percent). But less than half attend weekly religious services of any kind (41 percent), and only 8 percent would cite a religious leader as a role model.[4] The largest single religious category in the Harvard Crimson's 'by the numbers' survey of the class of 2019 was 'agnostic' (21.3 percent)."[5] One of the defining characteristics of Generation Z is that they are being raised by Generation X parents. Remember, these are the adults who follow four rules: be skeptical; rewrite the rules; accept "true for you but not for me"; embrace life and family over work. As a result, Generation Z children are typically self-directed and independent. They are empowered to choose their own extra curricular activities, preferred learning style, and even spiritual path. As a result, spiritually, Generation Z is open to experimentation and many truths.

Beyond the trends above, according to the marketing research of Sparks and Honey, here are the top "Z" headlines:[6]

- They are eager to start working.
- They are mature and in control.
- They intend to change the world.
- They've learned that traditional choices don't guarantee success.
- Entrepreneurship is in their DNA.
- They seek education and knowledge, and they use social media as a research tool.
- They multitask across five screens, and their attention spans are getting shorter.

- They think spatially and in 4D but lack situational awareness.
- They communicate with symbols, speed, and images.
- Their social circles are global.
- They are hyperaware and concerned about humanity's impact on the planet.
- They are less active and frequently obese.
- They live stream and co-create.

Questions for Reflection

1. What do you appreciate most about Generation Z?

2. What questions do you have for this generation?

3. What was the most surprising finding about Generation Z to you? Why? And what does it mean for your ministry?

4. Generation Z is the largest generation alive today. Those in this generation will not simply influence American culture; they will define American culture. How does that reality impact the way you view Generation Z?

Section 3

LESSONS FROM INNOVATIVE ORGANIZATIONS

In this section we'll highlight some of our favorite innovative organizations in the United States (Facebook, Starbucks, Uber, Netflix, and Disney) who are demonstrating deep understanding, relational ability, and impact with younger generations. Millennials are the least churched adult generation and the least likely to either identify as Christian or say faith is very important to their life.[1] As a result, looking outside the church for understanding and effective strategy is essential.

These organizations were not chosen because they are examples of perfection nor do they have the same mission as the church. They all have unique missions and visions. They were not chosen because they are examples of holy morals. Each organization has strengths and weaknesses. Yet, they were chosen because each is an example of a passionate pursuit of its mission, intentional systems for reaching its customers, and risk taking in the face of uncertainty. As a result, we can learn from their experiences.

Chapter 6

FACEBOOK:
BUILDING COMMUNITY
AND BRINGING THE
WORLD CLOSER
TOGETHER

Some Christians remember the moment they professed Jesus Christ as Savior or joined the church as a moment of new life. Moms remember the moment their children were born as a moment of new life. And the day people became connected with the world through social media also can be counted as a moment of new life for many. When connected on social media, suddenly people go from sharing pictures of life privately in their photo app, via email, or in printed books to instantly sharing a public profile with pictures and posts with the world along with thousands of "friends." Take a look at someone's Facebook profile and you'll probably know more about them than some members of their own family.

On February 4, 2004, Mark Zuckerberg launched a new website called "The Facebook." He named the site after the directories that were handed out to boarding school and university students to help them get to know one another better. Membership to the website was at first restricted to Harvard students. In 2004 and

2005, Zuckerberg and a team expanded the site to additional universities, colleges, and high schools. And finally, in September of 2006, Facebook announced that anyone who was at least thirteen years old and had a valid email address could join.[1] That included people across all generations from Traditionalists to Boomers, Generation X to Millennials.

Today, Facebook is the world's most-used social networking service with 1.4 billion daily active users, and 2.13 billion monthly active users as of December 31, 2017.[2] That's massive!

Facebook's mission is to give people the power to build community and bring the world closer together. People use Facebook to stay connected with friends and family, to discover what's going on in the world, and to share and express what matters to them. In many ways this mission is similar to that of the church. The church also envisions building community and bringing the world closer through discipleship. Unfortunately, the church is sometimes more of a social club than a place where new people find friends and grow deep in discipleship.

In light of the challenges of community and connection here are some of the biggest lessons we've learned from our experience engaging with others using Facebook. These are important for the church and any organization that seeks to reach younger and more diverse people.

1. Online Community Matters.

We live in a GIFTY (Google, Instagram, Facebook, Twitter, YouTube) culture that loves "selfies" and values immediacy, authenticity, and transparency. Yet, we are also tempted to "filter" our lives and stifle progress toward one of our deepest needs as humans, which is true belonging. We long to be accepted by a family, a community, or an organization that knows us by name, loves us unconditionally, and helps us to find meaning and hope in life. We want to belong to groups where joys are experienced, meals are shared, and "good news" is lived out. This belonging sometimes happens in the context of a local church and sometimes not. Facebook is seeking to fill the void of community where the church has failed.

While the vast physical, mental, and spiritual needs of people cannot solely be fulfilled virtually, the numbers don't lie. 1.4 billion people are connecting with Facebook each day globally. This includes 214 million users in the United States as of January 2018.[3] Of these, 58.3 million are between twenty-five and thirty-four years old. In 2017, US users spent an average of forty-one minutes on the site each day.[4] According to a study published in the Harvard Review, Facebook is also young peoples' social network of choice for an employer—almost 15 percent of Millennials stated that they would want to work for the online company (third overall after Google and Apple).[5] So online community matters and is not going away anytime soon. As a church we can either begrudge online platforms like Facebook or view them as tools to enable discipleship.

2. Vulnerable and Resilient Leadership Matters.

Everything at Facebook starts with Mark Zuckerberg, but it doesn't end there. As the co-founder and chief visionary for Facebook, Mark's impact is undeniable. He's personally demonstrated the values of risk taking, resilience, and reinvention. While there is an amazing team of talent around Mark (we'll talk about that later) his commitment to personally demonstrate these values are essential. And while other leaders at Facebook come and go, Mark's leadership presence for the past fourteen years is an essential element of the company's success especially in times when highly touted features or products have failed or risky decisions are made.

In 2006, when Facebook was barely two years old with $20 million dollars in revenue and 10 million users, Yahoo offered $1 billion to acquire the company. Up until that point a dozen offers had come from other companies to buy Facebook, but not for $1 billion dollars.

Mark Zuckerberg shared this perspective on risk-taking in an interview:

> 10 million people using the product at the time, so it wasn't as if it were obvious that we were going to succeed far beyond that, and that was the first point where we really had to look at the future and say, "Wow! Is what we're going to build going to actually be so much more meaningful for this?" And that caused a lot of interesting conversations in the company and with our investors, and at the end of that, Dustin and I just decided, "No, we think that we can actually go connect more than just the 10 million people who are in schools. We can go beyond that and have this really be a successful thing." And we just had to go for it, but that was really stressful because a lot of people really thought that we should sell the company.... But I think... since then, there have been much harder decisions that we've had to make where sometimes you have to bet on something and either bet the direction of the company or bet billions of dollars on something, and it's not going to be clear whether you're right for 5 or 10 years....[6]

Vulnerability includes acknowledging that some decisions may not be popular. It also means results may be uncertain and could result in being emotionally or physically harmed for those decisions. Yet, leadership requires decision making and risk taking. We make the best decisions for the time and trust that the outcomes will serve the highest and best good. As women, as persons of color, the risk of vulnerability can be particularly unnerving because the stakes seem higher. When decisions are made that are controversial, people in the minority stand out and there is often an added responsibility for one's community and family that are real. So knowing these risks and making the best decisions anyway is the essence of resilience. Resilience is what gives people the mental strength to cope with stress and hardship. It is the inner supply of strength that people are able to call on in times of need to carry them through. It's the ability to "bounce back" and keep moving toward the mission that's required for adaptive change even when others believe the mission is not achievable and seems too aspirational. Mark Zuckerberg is an example of this kind of resilience in action.

3. Investing in Relationships Online and Offline Matters.

One of the things Facebook has done exceptionally well is recruiting and hiring talented people regardless of age, tenure, gender, or ethnicity. When Mark started Facebook as a sophomore in college he had no experience running a technology company. So experience in a specific area is not the most important attribute for innovative organizations like Facebook. Mark said:

"So we invest in people who we think are just really talented, even if they haven't done that thing before. And that applies to people who are fresh out of university as well as people like the

CFO, who took the company public, had not taken a company public before...so just focusing on really talented people and creating opportunities for people. That also, I think, keeps the best people engaged and makes the best people want to come work at your company because they feel like, 'Oh, I'm going to get those kind of opportunities too.'"[7]

Deep belonging and commitment happens within supportive communities where people are given opportunities to grow and do work that transforms lives. This applies as much to a church with volunteers, within local schools, and within government as it does to a large tech company like Facebook. In fact, the church could be a leader in providing opportunities for meaningful work for younger generations.

A lot has been said about Millennials in the workplace. The words, "lazy," "unmotivated" and "slackers" have been quoted. However, our experience working directly with Millennials is very different. The reality is, Millennials—like most people—want to be engaged in creative and challenging work, receive consistent feedback on their work, and feel a part of a team. And according to a study by The Society for Human Resource Management, "94 percent of millennials want to use their skills to benefit a cause."[8] So what does that mean for the church? This means the most important resource that must be nurtured and multiplied is leadership.

4. Using Technology Well Matters.

With 1.5 billion users on Facebook the majority of our US communities and most church-goers are connected using social media. So gaining mastery in the strategy and execution of social media to create community is essential. Importantly, this is not the work of the pastor or lay leader alone. It requires a team, including Millennials and members of Generation Z (even though they may not use the same social media platforms that are familiar to older generations in your congregation). Here are three essentials as you build your social media presence:

Quality over quantity. If your goal is to represent your church, brand, or product on Facebook, creating a Facebook page is essential. A page allows you to engage with people on Facebook and offers tools to help you manage and track engagement. You can have an unlimited number of people following you, and you can follow up to five thousand people. Once you have a page, publishing quality content is essential. Remember *better* social media content, not necessarily *more* content is the goal. People's social media news feeds are noisy places with posts from friends and advertisements from marketers. In the midst of this noise, some churches might be tempted to promote every church meeting, event, and worship service. Yet, social media is not just about promoting. The primary purpose people are on social media is for *social* connection, not advertisement. So our first goal on social media must be encouraging, helping, or inspiring people with quality content not just quantity.

Timing is important. There are many social media hubs like Hootsuite and Buffer that can automatically post your social media posts at times when people can actually read them. Posting when your day slows down, in the middle of the night when you remember, or at other off times usually means low interaction—people just don't see them. Using a service to post on your behalf means that you will maximize your audience by ensuring that when your post hits the noisy social media feed, people will see it. If people see the post, your quality is good, and your content is helpful, they will interact with it. If the people interact with it, you maximize your audience because it is then shared across multiple networks, not just your own.

Use images to get your audience's attention. You many have heard that people only remember 10 percent of what we read, 20 percent of what we hear, 30 percent of what we see, 50 percent of what we see and hear, 70 percent of what we discuss with others, 80 percent of what we personally experience, and 95 percent of what we teach others after seventy-two hours. This comes from Edgar Dale's "Cone of Experience," developed in 1946 that provided an intuitive model of the concreteness of various audiovisual media.[9] Researchers have disputed the exactness of these numbers, but our experience is that engaging people using text, images, and live video is most effective.

Create Facebook groups to enable deeper engagement. Facebook groups bring together individuals who share a common interest. For example, small groups, mission teams, or worship committees could create their own Facebook groups to build community, share inspiration and information. Of the people on Facebook, many have identified the groups they belong to as "very meaningful"—communities that "quickly become the most important part of someone's experience on Facebook."[10]

Questions for Reflection

1. What do you appreciate most about Facebook's story?

2. What's the next courageous decision you feel called to make? What's the cost of *not* taking the risk?

3. How will you seek out a diverse group of the best and brightest in your community?

4. How can your congregation or organization use Facebook to more effectively build community?

Chapter 7

STARBUCKS: ONWARD TO MEMORABLE EXPERIENCES

One of the places we (Jasmine, Lia, and Rodney) love is Starbucks. We all live in different places and have different schedules, which makes it hard to catch up with each other in person. In fact on one of the first days that the three of us connected for the first time in the same physical location was on a cool Washington, DC, spring day where we made a Starbucks run for our favorite drinks. Our experience at Starbucks in places like DC, Atlanta, Kansas City, and St. Louis proves that savoring a simple cup of coffee (or Jasmine's signature favorite Chai Tea Latte) can connect people and create community among us. You can be sure that many hours of writing this book have taken place while drinking good coffee and tea from Starbucks.

While many stories have been written about "third places," or places beyond home and work where people gather and create community, Starbucks has a long record of working to perfect the experience. There is much we can all learn from its culture and practices. This chapter contains lessons from Starbucks that any thriving organization should stop, look, and learn from to thrive.

1. Admit Mistakes and Take a Step Back.

Since Starbucks launched in September 1971, we're sure it has experienced many moments of truth, but two stick out for us in particular. The first was in 2008, and the second was ten years later in 2018.

One Tuesday in February 2008, Starbucks closed all of its stores. A note posted on 7,100 locked doors explained the reason. "We're taking time to perfect our espresso. Great espresso requires practice. That's why we're dedicating ourselves to honing our craft."[1] While some might assume this wasn't that big of a deal, Howard Schultz, the CEO of Starbucks, was warned against closing all the stores across America. Yet, Schultz believed closing the stores at 5:30 p.m. on a Tuesday, perfecting the espresso-making process, and investing in Starbucks' people were so important that he was willing to take the risk. As predicted, Starbucks lost $6 million that evening and competitors targeted its customers. Closing stores and losing $6 million was not just a routine decision. It was big, bold, and value-driven decision. It was a galvanizing moment for Starbucks' partners and a symbol for other organizations and the world about the importance of people, trust, and excellence. Ten years after Starbucks' decision to take a step back to be able to go forward the Seattle-based coffee chain has more than doubled over the last decade to more than 27,000 stores worldwide and more than 13,000 in the United States in 2017.[2]

Where's your "espresso-like" moment of truth in your customer experience? Where are higher standards needed in your church, conference, or organization? Where is courageous conviction essential today?

A decade later, on Tuesday in May 28, 2018, Starbucks once again closed its doors to 8,000 stores. A note on its website homepage read, "We'll see you tomorrow. Our stores (and mobile ordering) are closing this afternoon. We are closing early as our teams reconnect with our mission and each other."[3] Starbucks closed 8,000 stores in the United States for companywide anti-bias training, for 175,000 employees. The training is part of an effort to improve its behavior toward customers, its image, and impact on the communities it serves after the arrests to two African American men in a Starbucks in Philadelphia who were waiting for a friend inside a Starbucks store in April 2018. Starbucks apologized for the incident, terminated the employee who called the police, and admitted that this was an experience of racial bias. Starbucks' training focused on how employees can better assess their own assumptions and biases, help improve customer service, and ideally prevent incidents like the one in Philadelphia.[4] While anti-bias training will not eliminate racism, it can facilitate conversation between employees to build greater understanding, trust, and hopefully customer outcomes.

Frank Dobbin, a sociology professor at Harvard University, who has studied diversity education efforts says, "Arranging anti-bias training is a very common reaction when a firm gets negative press about race or gender relations.... You can't change people's attitudes through a short-term intervention." Instead, Professor Dobbin suggested that Starbucks try to diversify its stores by developing special recruitment guidelines, mentoring programs and regional task forces. "The best thing they could do, the thing that's been most effective in all the studies I know of, is to fully integrate all the different levels of the organization so that white male managers are working alongside black female managers, where people work alongside people from other groups and get to know them."[5]

Starbucks is an example for churches and other organizations to learn from.

2. Decide to Be the Best.

In 2008 Starbucks was plagued by the US financial recession like many other consumer companies. Sales growth and new store openings significantly slowed. Howard Schulz returned as CEO in an attempt to resurrect Starbucks to its previous glory. The company's "very survival was at stake."[6] Led by Schulz, Starbucks developed its "Transformation Agenda" beginning with this aspirational vision statement: "To become an enduring, great company with one of the most recognized and respected brands in the world, known for inspiring and nurturing the human spirit."[7] What's clear in this vision is Starbucks' desire to be a great company with a great brand while doing good. Likewise, Starbucks also knew it could neither transform the company, nor the world, if it did not excel and lead in its primary business or, "Be the undisputed coffee authority."[8] This was the first of its seven strategic priorities. Simultaneously, the seventh of the priorities was to "Deliver a sustainable economic model."[9] Starbucks knew it could not deliver the other priorities of the strategic agenda without a profitable business model.

3. Create Memorable Experiences.

As we reflect on why we love Starbucks, we realize that it's about more than coffee. Three words that describe our experience are comfort, connection, and contribution. Starbucks is one of the places where the smell of coffee beans and view of deep brown hues slow our souls for a few minutes during busy days.

It's a place where we feel connected to friends across the world, knowing that they are having a similar experience as they work, rest, and practice creativity. We are inspired by the contribution of Starbucks knowing the coffee beans are ethically sourced and jobs are created, partners from diverse backgrounds are valued, and social consciousness is nurtured. This makes our hearts strangely warm and spurs us to spend $5 for a cup of tea or espresso pretty regularly. Starbucks' goal is to become the "third place" in our daily lives (i.e. Home, Work, and Starbucks). Baristas call you by your name. It provides the comfort of a home office, connection of good friends, and contribution to the world . . . oh, and a personalized experience as well.

Third places is a term coined by sociologist Ray Oldenburg and refers to places where people spend time between home ("first" place) and work ("second" place). They are places where people exchange ideas, have a good time, and build relationships.[10] For many Americans, third places are as likely to be virtual as in person—from Facebook to Snapchat to FaceTime to group texts. But as Oldenburg notes, "the most effective third places for building real community seem to be physical places where people can easily and routinely connect with each other: churches, parks, recreation centers, barbershops, hairdressers, gyms and even fast-food restaurants."[11]

Starbucks is not perfect in execution by any measure, but we have come to admire its commitment to core values evidenced by the customer experience first, its partners second, and then the community. This three-pronged approach continues to inspire many across the globe. "I'll take a Grande hazelnut latte, extra hot, with skim milk please." "May I have a Grande Chai with peppermint, almond milk, no water, extra hot and no foam, please?" "I don't speak Starbucks but that sounds good. I'll have what Jasmine's having. Thanks." What's your order?

Questions for Reflection

1. Like Starbucks' espresso quality, where is the moment of truth for your congregation or organization?

2. What mistakes need to be admitted to go forward?

3. What could you be the best at in the world?

4. What kind of experiences are you creating for your customers? What customer data indicates your effectiveness?

5. How is your congregation creating a place for new people to create community, build relationships, and grow in discipleship?

6. Where is greater diversity and inclusion needed in your congregation or organization? Where could additional training and mentoring related to diversity help?

Chapter 8

UBER:
THE VISION IS BIGGER
THAN WE THOUGHT

W e remember our first shared Uber ride. We were headed from downtown Washington, DC, to the airport after three days of stimulating, yet exhausting, discussions on public policy and theology. We were tutored on the app, but were still feeling nervous about trusting this airport ride to an unfamiliar experience. But we took a leap of faith, trusted others' wisdom, and dashed off to the airport. The car was clean and the driver was polite. In twenty-five minutes we arrived at the airport without incident. The driver grabbed our bags from the trunk as we exited the car and headed to our gates. We exhaled. It was an unexpectedly easy experience. We were officially indoctrinated into the "Uber economy"[1] and we haven't looked back since. This chapter contains lessons from Uber's disruptive business model from which any thriving organization can learn.

1. Intangible Assets Matter.

Uber owns none of its cars. Its other tangible assets, like offices, iPhones, and computers, are minimal. But it does own very significant technology, including software and customer data. It also has deep customer relationships because of its data sharing technology. In this new intangible economy, organizations that possess intangible assets, such as leaders who can organize and connect with people well, talented artists, and computer programmers will be in great demand. Customers will choose to do business with the companies who provide the best customer experience. Likewise, workers are choosing companies that honor the diversity of their work styles and preferences. For example, ordained minister Kenneth Drayton has turned his 2009 Mercury Grand Marquis into a church-on-wheels, transforming his car into a sanctuary for himself and his passengers. "The job lets me open the door into my passengers' lives," said Drayton, fifty-four, who said his Brooklyn trips often turn into therapy sessions. "The hope is to brighten their day and give them advice." The religious experience happens the moment a passenger plops down in the backseat, Drayton said, "I only play classical music, my car is immaculately clean, and they can sense the presence of God," he said, adding that passengers are immersed in "peace and tranquility." Passengers quickly open up and bear their challenges.[2] What if a future church mirrors the mission of Uber becoming mobile and bringing spirituality—for everyone, everywhere.

2. Mission Must Be Multifaceted.

Uber's mission to bring transportation—for everyone, everywhere—was founded in 2009 to solve an important problem: How do you get a ride at the push of a button? More than five billion trips later, Uber is tackling even greater challenges: making transportation safer with self-driving cars, delivering food quickly and affordably with Uber Eats, and reducing congestion in cities by getting more people into fewer cars.[3] Clearly, Uber's mission goes beyond transportation. It's driving disruptive change in ways from which we can learn.

For example, Uber is "Driving Change By Connecting with the Communities It Serves."[4] As part of Uber's ongoing commitment to drive change and help prevent sexual assault and domestic violence in global communities, it's teaming up with leading organizations for a sexual assault awareness and prevention initiative. In partnership with national partners NO MORE, RALIANCE, the National Network to End Domestic Violence, A CALL TO MEN, Casa de Esperanza, Women of Color Network, Inc., and the National Coalition of Anti-Violence Program, Uber hosted fifty Community Forums Across the United States with prevention advocates, corporate leaders, members of the public, and riders and drivers.[5] These events provided local communities with a forum for open, diverse discussions around sexual assault prevention, education, and resources. One of the policy changes Uber has initiated is "Trusted Contacts: Riders will be able to designate up to five friends and family members as Trusted Contacts, and be prompted to share trip details with them during every ride. This makes it easier than ever to share your trip, so loved ones can follow along and know when you've arrived. Prefer to share your trip during evening rides only? Night time sharing will be an option."[6]

These initiatives have been developed in part due to feedback from Uber riders and drivers. While Uber has faced challenges, its response has been rooted in community conversation, collaboration, and policy change.

3. Find New Ways to Reach New People.

In spring, 2018 Uber introduced Uber Health as a tool to remove transportation as a barrier to healthcare. Uber writes,

> Whether it's helping seniors regain their independence, providing newfound mobility to those living in underserved areas, or providing a safe alternative to drinking and driving, Uber has changed the way people live their lives in ways that were never expected. Yet, still, there's so much more that can be done. We're unveiling a new service focused on an issue vital to all of us: health. Every year, 3.6 million Americans miss doctor appointments due to a lack of reliable transportation. No-show rates are as high as 30 percent nationwide. And while transportation barriers are common across the general population, these barriers are greatest for vulnerable populations, including patients with the highest burden of chronic disease.[7]

Uber is a transportation company that deeply understands its customers from people needing rides to work, partiers who want to avoid drinking and driving to seniors and vulnerable adults who need reliable, comfortable transportation to medical appointments. Importantly, Uber is not just offering its typical ride service, it's partnering with health care professionals to order rides for patients to ensure they don't miss appointments. Not only is this innovation a benefit to patients, and caregivers, it's a new revenue stream for Uber.

Interestingly, Uber has even shifted its technology to meet the needs of the patient and health care professionals. Coordinators can schedule rides on behalf of patients weeks in advance, and access is available for patients without a smartphone. Patients don't need the Uber app, or even a smartphone, to get a ride with Uber Health because it's all done through text message. For many, their first ever Uber ride will be through Uber Health.[8]

Uber has revolutionized the way we move, disrupted previous business models, and keeps expanding by solving customer problems. Uber provides new and expandable forms of income and financial sustainability for individuals while creating flexibility for work and personal schedules. Who knows what's next, but we're excited to take the ride.

Questions for Reflection

1. What do you appreciate most about Uber's story?

2. What questions do you have about Uber?

3. What lessons gleaned from Uber's experience are most important for the church today? How can we apply them to the local church today?

4. How are you being called to take your mission more mobile, for everyone, everywhere?

5. How is your mission multifaceted to impact your community and its people positively, not just your church or organization's goals?

6. Uber also provides new and expandable forms of income with flexibility to meet work and personal schedules. How can the church welcome adaptive scheduling to accommodate new and expanding work schedules and income producing entities?

Chapter 9

NETFLIX: DISRUPT, CUSTOMIZE, DIVERSIFY

Lia: Personal confession, I might be the last person on the planet to try Netflix...

Jas: Really... *What took you so long!?*

Lia: Idk... do I really need another internet show thing... I already have YouTube Premium and Amazon Prime.

Jas: *Geezzz...No comparison...Different platforms for different content.*

Lia: Okay...just got the 1 month free trial. Whooo!

Jas:

Netflix was just named one of the 2018 World's Most Innovative Companies by *Fast Company Magazine*. It also debuted a new commercial during the Black Entertainment TV (BET) Awards in 2018, on its commitment to hire and cast black talent. The media hype caught our attention so we decided to check out what all the excitement is about.

Netflix is a $62 billion public entertainment company specializing in online on-demand streaming video, as well as a

DVD-by-mail service. It was founded in Scotts Valley, California, in 1997 and began its current subscription model in 1999.[1] Well before the proliferation of subscription services like Amazon Prime and YouTube Premium, Netflix disrupted the video entertainment industry and displaced traditional video businesses like Blockbuster Video. A story is told that the idea for Netflix was birthed after one of the cofounders paid $40 in late fees to Blockbuster on one video![2] Now according to its YouTube page the company has over 125 million members across the 190 countries watching millions of hours of original and licensed TV shows and movies every day.[3] Netflix's revolution is inspiring as we consider innovation for the church. Here are three key lessons.

1. Disrupt Yourself.

Three years after its founding in 2000, a start-up called Netflix was turned down for investment by the $6 billion category leader Blockbuster. A decade later in 2010 Blockbuster went bankrupt and Netflix now has 125 million subscribers. The moral of the story? Innovation is happening all around us whether we want to admit it or not. Netflix co-founder Randolph advises, "If you're not prepared to disrupt yourself, if you're not constantly innovating and changing and trying to stay current, then you are leaving the door wide open for someone to come and disrupt that category for you."[4] So how do you figure out how to disrupt yourself? Randolph suggests, "Look for pain. You have to train yourself to see everything as imperfect and ask yourself: 'what's wrong'? Look at things closer to home that you know well. Processes with dealing with customers, processes you do every day at work. What frustrates you? What do you bump into that's a problem?"

Randolph cites the design of the humble paint can, which hasn't been updated in forty years and remains difficult and inefficient to use as the perfect example. The paint can is just waiting for someone to disrupt and innovate it.[5]

2. Customize: One Size Does Not Fit All.

Unlike traditional broadcasters, Netflix's goal isn't to appeal to as broad an audience as possible but rather to cater to niches and effectively give every slice of the population a show or movie they can't live without. As a result, Netflix is widely considered to be a liberal media source because it's intentionally offering programming targeted by affinity. For example, in December 2016, it rolled out technology that offers custom-created preview videos that automatically play when you scroll over a title card based on the kind of content the user likes to watch. The redesign encourages Netflix's subscribers easily to discover new shows to watch rather than tediously browse its catalog and encounter hundreds of interesting options.

When new users sign up for Netflix one of the first steps to complete after inputting an email address is to choose which shows they like. After selecting three shows, similar shows popped up that the Netflix algorithm thinks they'd enjoy. Nice! The elimination of uninteresting content simplifies life.

3. Diversify: Race and Inclusion Matter.

A powerful example of Netflix's commitment to diversity and inclusion is the commercial titled "A Great Day In Hollywood."[6] The advertisement was inspired by the 1958 photograph "A Great Day in Harlem" featuring fifty-seven jazz legends—including

Charles Mingus, Thelonious Monk, and Count Basie—on the stairs of a New York brownstone snapped by photographer Art Kane.[7] Netflix is leading the way representing a movement where black people are getting more leading roles within the Netflix platform and the broader entertainment industry. The commercial featured forty-seven talented black actors from genres as diverse as comedy to drama to science fiction.

The Netflix organization is not without its challenges related to diversity. In June 2018, "the abrupt departure of corporate communications chief Jonathan Friedland for what the company described as his 'descriptive use of the N-word on at least two occasions at work'" was disturbing.[8] Netflix CEO Rex Hastings wrote:

> There is not a way to neutralize the emotion and history behind the word in any context. The use of the phrase "N-word" was created as a euphemism, and the norm, with the intention of providing an acceptable replacement and moving people away from using the specific word. When a person violates this norm, it creates resentment, intense frustration, and great offense for many.... Going forward, we are going to find ways to educate and help our employees broadly understand the many difficult ways that race, nationality, gender identity and privilege play out in society and our organization. We seek to be great at inclusion, across many dimensions, and these incidents show we are uneven at best. We have already started to engage outside experts to help us learn faster.

Our hope is that Netflix's experience provides a wake-up call to the church and our communities. While we'd hope individual and systemic racial bias no longer exists, it does, and it calls for us to acknowledge, repent, and reconcile. As a church, our call is to appreciate diversity and practice radical inclusion.

Questions for Reflection

1. What do you appreciate most about Netflix's story?

2. What questions do you have about Netflix?

3. What pain are people feeling in your community? What frustrates you? That's the beginning of an opportunity to innovate.

4. What lessons gleaned from Netflix's experience are most important for the church today? How can we apply them to the local church?

Chapter 10

A DISNEY EXPERIENCE

Many of the growing companies of today are clear that their businesses are not just delivering a service, but creating a memorable experience. Airbnb's mission is to help customers "book unique homes and experiences all over the world."[1] Uber's mission is to "bring transportation—for everyone, everywhere."[2] These both speak not just to providing beds to sleep in or cars to ride in, but to a customized experience wherever you are.

Maybe your church has updated its lobby, added contemporary music, and started new small groups to better attract and meet the needs of younger generations. Yet, to realize the full benefit of remarkable experiences, organizations must deliberately design engaging experiences that are perceived as intrinsically valuable. This transition from providing services to creating experiences will not be easy for established churches to undertake, but is essential for vital organizations in the twenty-first and twenty-second centuries.

When was the last time you had a truly remarkable experience that you felt was designed especially for you? One of the times we experienced an extraordinary time was when we visited Walt Disney World in Orlando, Florida, on a family vacation. Disney World has the incredible ability to turn every vacation into a "once in a lifetime experience." For our family this started during the planning of the vacation, and continued as we left the real world behind and surrendered ourselves to the magic that Disney seemed to have created just for us. Here are four reasons that make Disney World in Orlando, Florida, a favorite vacation experience for people across the world.

1. Convenient Transportation

Disney makes it convenient and easy to get wherever you need to go from the airport to the property—and beyond. The airport shuttle and luggage delivery service provided by Disney's Magical Express began the magic as soon as we arrived. We didn't have to hassle with renting a car or waiting for an Uber. The Magical Express was waiting to greet us and dozens of other excited guests. Let the party begin! On the resort, a fleet of buses makes travel to the parks and resorts a breeze—one that comes around at least once every ten to twenty minutes.

2. The Immersive Experience

Wherever you go on Disney property, Disney has created a storyline for you to follow. From the theming of the resorts to the interactive rides at the parks, that attention to detail immerses you in the fun in a way that truly brings the story to life. Our immersion included meeting favorite Disney characters like Mickey and Minnie to kid favorites like Cinderella, Sofia the First, Buzz Lightyear, and Doc McStuffins. It continued with the pristine cleanliness and smiles of the staff that keep everything looking fresh and inviting. Instead of being secondary, Disney's ability to sprinkle even our wait in line with a little bit of inspiration and fun built anticipation while making time pass much more quickly.

3. Convenience and "Meals Included"

Disney World has built itself a reputation as a destination for good food along side the theme park fun. With everything from the standard fare such as burgers and chicken fingers to more gourmet options like Herb-Crusted Lamb and Cedar Plank Blackened Salmon, there is something available for everyone. Our kiddos loved the resort food court that has everything from pizza and pasta to burgers and fries. The meals were included in our resort package, and the kids could choose what they wanted. And all the ice cream they could eat!

4. Spectacular Opening Ceremonies and Fireworks Finales

Beginning the day with the opening ceremonies with smiling character faces as they welcome you to the most magical place on earth is spectacular. Capping off the day with the unforgettable sights and sounds of brilliant light shows and thrilling performances is an unexpected delight. The intentionality of beginnings and endings really do make any visit to Disney World memorable.

Disney's Four Keys[3] are the guiding principles through which each Disney "experience" is designed. They provide the laser focus which each "cast member" is responsible to embody. These four keys lead to consistency and shared priority in the organization.

Safety

In order to create a safe and relaxing place, safety of Guests and also Cast comes before anything else.

85

Courtesy

Based on the belief that Guests should be treated like VIPs, we also aspire to offer friendly, genuine hospitality; not just being polite but providing service from the standpoint of the Guests.

Show

Cast Members are part of the show and should treat every day as the opening day, approaching every task as part of a themed show, even when they are inspecting or cleaning the facilities.

Efficiency

Focusing on safety, courtesy and the show will, along with teamwork, help us achieve greater efficiency.

Disney is an example of designing a remarkable experience with the people you hope to reach at the center, not the experienced Disney guest or the staff, but the first-time guest is the priority. Disney is intentional to ensure first-time guests have an unforgettable experience and want to return. New guests are the first priority followed by return guests.

Questions for Reflection

1. What do you appreciate most about the Disney experience?

2. How might your hospitality be enhanced in light of the Disney experience?

3. How might your worship be enhanced in light of the Disney experience?

4. How might your community interactions be enhanced in light of the Disney experience?

Section 4

CREATING NEW MODELS OF MINISTRY WITH MILLENNIALS AND GENERATION Z AT THE CENTER USING A HUMAN-CENTERED DESIGN

Human-centered design is all about building a deep empathy with the people you're designing for; generating tons of ideas; building a bunch of prototypes; sharing what you've made with the people you're designing for; and eventually putting your innovative new solution out in the world.[1]

In this section, we dive into how to use the "blank slate." The metaphor of a "blank slate" comes from the words *tabula rasa,* meaning, "the mind in its hypothetical primary blank or empty state before receiving outside impressions."[2] We are all born with a blank slate, meaning that at birth, all humans are born with the ability to become literally anything or anyone. Yet, our life experiences and socialization impacts who and what we actually become. Likewise, if we can strip away previous assumptions, fears, and cultural stereotypes we can shift mindsets, create new experiences, and shape the future of the church no matter what the current state. We invite you into a blank slate using design thinking as a model to create innovative solutions to problems. We invite you—no, implore you—to look beyond quick, easy, temporary fixes and engage with innovative Millennial and Generation Z partners. After all, these are the younger generations we seek to reach.

In today's world the best organizations are shifting from just providing services to creating memorable experiences. As a result, organizations that were once commodities are differentiating themselves, growing in impact, and connecting with new generations. America Online's (AOL) instant messaging (AIM) was the leader in online communication for years. AIM is now officially dead because it did not innovate and provide the kind of real time, easy access, GIF- and Meme-loving platform that text messaging did. Text messaging started with 140 characters of tapping for forever on your phone to get to the correct letter or number. Yet, it evolved into the experiential way of communicating that it is now. Will it last? Ask Snapchat or FaceTime...

With this blank slate, the kind of action we're calling for is a new kind of innovative leadership that reaches across generations, lifestyles, and cultures. Importantly, this kind of leadership is the call of every person, not just religious professionals. In the role of spiritual leader, a person chooses to be immersed in the world and in God. She loves humanity and Jesus. He seeks diverse relationships with people and deliberately takes times away from people to be with God. This leader is led by a deep knowing that the pandemonium of life does not have the last word. This blank slate leader realizes that we are courageously living in between times of sadness and joy, turmoil and peace, disbelief and eternal hope. Importantly, at our best, leaders bear their souls through the sharing of personal stories so others may see the enduring qualities of God, experience courage, and remain hopeful despite their circumstances.

Design thinking, or human-centered design, is a way to create innovative solutions to problems while inviting the people you're trying to reach to the center. In particular, for businesses that are service based, like the church, design thinking is all about creating remarkable experiences with Millennials and Generation Z at the center because these are the new generations we seek to reach. We know the design for an experience is truly great when it stands out as an impactful and remarkable experience, not just a good service.

An example of this cultural shift is found in the evolution of the birthday cake as cited in a *Harvard Business Review* article. It states:

"The entire history of economic progress can be recapitulated in the four-stage evolution of the birthday cake. As a vestige of the agrarian economy, mothers made birthday cakes from scratch, mixing farm commodities (flour, sugar, butter, and eggs) that together cost mere dimes. As the goods-based industrial economy advanced, moms paid a dollar or two to Betty Crocker for premixed ingredients. Later, when the service economy took hold, busy parents ordered cakes from the bakery or grocery store, which, at $10 or $15, cost ten times as much as the packaged ingredients. Now, in the time-starved 1990s, parents neither make the birthday cake nor even throw the party. Instead, they spend $100 or more to "outsource" the entire event to Chuck E. Cheese's, the Discovery Zone, the Mining Company, or some other business that stages a memorable event for the kids—and often throws in the cake for free. Welcome to the emerging *experience economy.*"[3]

In this section we'll introduce a model that puts Millennials and Generation Z at the center using human-centered design and the Mission Possible game from The United Methodist Church Path 1 Team.[4] Our objective will be to design a solution to a social or ministry challenge using the tools of collaboration, mapping, concept creation, prototyping, and more to support this creative space. Let's play!

GAME TIME!

In ninety minutes we'll play an adaptation of the Mission Possible Game[1] to tackle challenging ministry and social problems using resources you already have. Use your creativity, collaboration, and playful energy to brainstorm ways to better serve your community, reinvigorate your mission, and create new ministries to reach new generations. This is a model you'll be able to take back to your congregation or organization and use over and over again.

In this experience, we will take a seemingly impossible mission to tackle, and use this game to create a possible solution to address the problem with Millennials and Generation Z at the center.

You'll begin by understanding and narrowing the scope of the problem. We live in a world where we can learn more about the problems facing us than ever before. Yet, the volume of information and alternative facts can make us feel like the problem is too big and too complex to solve. We feel hopeless. An antidote to this feeling of hopelessness is engagement in the problem-solving process. When people collaborate in problem identification and solutions they feel:

- important and significant
- competent and capable
- liked and accepted[2]

By the end of this experience you should be inspired and better equipped to think creatively about the issues you and your community are frustrated and passionate about. You'll also be able to design your own innovative solution to a social or ministry issue in your congregation and community.

Ground Rules

Gather into teams of three to five people with at least three generations represented, including at least people who are Millennials or Gen Z. You will need to work together as a team to construct a solution to a problem.

Pick one person to take notes as you answer the questions that follow as a team.

Pick another person to present your team's solution to the rest of the room. At the end of the game someone from each team will present the solution to the rest of the room and allow other teams to ask questions.

9 Design Thinking Steps (Adapted from the Path 1 Mission Possible Game)

To order the actual game, see the weblink in the endnote. These instructions have been adapted with permission by UMC Discipleship Ministries and Path 1.[3]

- Understand the problem.
- Refine the problem.
- Ask what resources you have.
- Ideate!
- Collaborate.

- Assess impact.
- Decide next steps.
- Test, evaluate, refine.
- Give feedback.

1. Choose a Problem to Address. (five minutes)

For this exercise, choose *one* problem from the list below to work on with your group of three to six people.

- job wages
- health care
- child poverty

A. Wages in the United States

- Minimum Wage: Since 2009, the federal minimum wage in the United States has remained at $7.25 per hour ranking eleventh among industrialized countries and fully $3.65 per hour less (in inflation adjusted dollars) than the minimum wage in 1968. And, the federal minimum has lost about 9.6 percent of its purchasing power to inflation.[4]

- Women's Wages: American women earn $0.83 on the dollar compared with men. Within the American workforce, there are many gaps in earnings between demographic groups, including by race and ethnicity.[5]

- Scripture: "How terrible for Jehoiakim, who builds his house with corruption and his upper chambers with injustice, working his countrymen for nothing, refusing to give them their wages" (Jeremiah 22:13). "Listen! Hear the cries of the wages of your field hands. These are the wages you stole from those who harvested your fields. The cries of the harvesters have reached the ears of the Lord of heavenly forces" (James 5:4).

- What does The United Methodist Church say? Throughout scripture, God commands us to treat workers with respect, dignity, and fairness. Exploitation or underpayment of workers is incompatible with Christ's commandment to love our neighbor—a love that extends to all persons in all places, including the workplace (2016 *Book of Resolutions*, #4101, "Living Wage Model").

B. Health Care in the United States

- In 2016, 28.1 million people in the United States lacked health insurance, a decrease of 0.3 percent from 2015. Most uninsured are in low-income working families.[6]

- In 2016, the uninsured rate for children under age nineteen in poverty, 7 percent, was higher than the uninsured rate for children not in poverty, 5 percent.

- People who don't have health insurance are more likely to forego preventive care, rely on the emergency room for care, be diagnosed in the late stages of a disease, and leave prescriptions unfilled.

- Scripture: "God created humanity in God's own image, in the divine image God created them, male and female God created them" (Genesis 1:27). "Promote the welfare of the city where I have sent you. . . . Pray to the LORD for it, because your future depends on its welfare" (Jeremiah 29:7). The Lord "who gives justice to people who are oppressed, who gives bread to people who are starving! The LORD: who frees prisoners. The LORD: who makes the blind see. The LORD: who straightens up those who are bent low. The LORD: who loves the righteous" (Psalm

146:7-8). "I came that they might have life—indeed, so that they could live life to the fullest" (John 10:10).

- What does The United Methodist Church say? "Health care is a basic human right" (Social Principles ¶162.V). "Health is a condition of physical, mental, social, and spiritual well-being" (Social Principles ¶162.V).

C. Child Poverty in the United States

- The United States has the second highest child poverty rate among thirty-five industrialized countries despite having the largest economy in the world. There are 14.7 million poor children and 6.5 million extremely poor children in the United States of America.[7]

- A child in the United States has a one in five chance of being poor, and the younger he or she is the poorer he or she is likely to be. A child of color, who will be in the majority of US children in 2020, is more than twice as likely to be poor as a white child.[8]

- Child poverty creates gaps in cognitive skills in babies. Poor parents have fewer financial resources and often experience more stress. As a result their young children are less likely to be read to, less likely to spend time talking to adults, and hear many fewer words each week than children from more affluent families. One study found that by age four, high-income children had heard 30 million more words than poor children. Poor preschoolers are also less likely to be able to recognize letters, count to twenty, or write their first names. Income-related gaps in cognitive skills can be observed in babies as early as nine months old and often widen with age. These disparities create an early disadvantage that is often hard to overcome.[9]

- Scripture: Matthew 25:37-40: "Then those who are righteous will reply to him, 'Lord, when did we see you hungry and feed you, or thirsty and give you a drink? When did we see you as a stranger and welcome you, or naked and give you clothes to wear? When did we see you sick or in prison and visit you?' Then the king will reply to them, 'I assure you that when you have done it for one of the least of these brothers and sisters of mine, you have done it for me.'"

- What does The United Methodist Church say? As a church, we are called to support the poor and challenge the rich. To begin to alleviate poverty, we support such policies as: adequate income maintenance, quality education, decent housing, job training, meaningful employment opportunities, adequate medical and hospital care, humanization and radical revisions of welfare programs, work for peace in conflict areas and efforts to protect creation's integrity (UMC Social Principles ¶163.E).[10]

2. Understand the Problem. (ten minutes)

Thomas Lockwood in his book, *Design Thinking*, identifies that the first key tenet of design thinking is to identify the right problem to solve, coupled with a deep understanding of the person or persons the problem affects.[11] This is achieved through observation, deep listening, research, and fieldwork with the persons you're trying to reach. For this reason great design thinking always begins with a focus on a person or group of people and their experiences, contexts, joys, challenges, and desires. Importantly, "when it comes to solving problems, the best results come about from digging as deeply as possible into the problem to find the root cause."[12]

Did you know this was a problem? What surprises you about this problem? What frustrates you? What firsthand experience do you have with this problem? What assumptions to you have about this problem? What are the root causes of this problem from the people's perspective?

Notes:

3. Refine the Problem. (five minutes)

Now that you understand the problem refine your focus. What part of this problem do you want to focus on? Where could you have the greatest impact in your community? Whose life would you like to impact? Write a statement of the problem you are solving.

Notes:

4. What Resources Do You Already Have? (five minutes)

Sometimes the resources you have shape the solutions. Sometimes the solutions you come up with shape the resources you'll use. Either way, you'll need to be resourceful and creative.

What resources (facilities, places, people, financial, equipment, etc.) do you already have or could easily acquire to help solve your problem? How could you more creatively use your resources?

Write a summary of your resources here.

Notes:

5. Develop Your Ideas! (twenty minutes)

Use the resources you have to create ideas to solve your problem. You could start a new program, launch a social enterprise, design an art show, invent a new product, pen a song, perform a show or much more. Remember, anything is possible at this stage. Brainstorm a list of possibilities without evaluating them. After you have a list, choose the one or two ideas you want to actualize using the criteria of resources and impact.

Write a summary of your solution here.

"Human-centered designers are unlike other problem solvers—we tinker and test, we fail early and
often, and we spend a surprising amount of time
not knowing the answer to the challenge at hand.
And yet, we forge ahead. We're optimists and mak-
ers, experimenters and learners, we empathize and
iterate, and we look for inspiration in unexpected
places. We believe that a solution is out there and
that by keeping focused on the people we're designing for and asking the right questions, we'll get there
together. We dream up lots of ideas, some that work
and some that don't. We make our ideas tangible so
that we can test them, and then we refine them. In
the end, our approach amounts to wild creativity, to
a ceaseless push to innovate, and a confidence that
leads us to solutions we'd never dreamed of when
we started."[13]

6. Collaborate as a Team. (ten minutes)

In design thinking you are not limited to your own resources,
structure, or roles. Rather, consider with whom you can partner to
bring your solution to life internally and externally. With whom
could you work that has similar values, vision, or mission? Who
would be your ideal partners? Who are sources of knowledge, skill,
or experience that could support your solution? Whom should
you contact first (key influencers)?

Importantly, human-centered design works best with diverse
teams. You could put three pastors together to work on a new
social enterprise, but if you throw a graphic designer, a journalist,
or an industrial designer into the mix, you're going to bring new
modes of thinking to your team. You could put three long time
Christians who are of the Baby Boomer generation together to

work on a new ministry idea, but if you throw in a Millennial sports enthusiast, a Gen Z who loves to draw, and a Gen X marketing expert into the mix, you're going to bring new modes of thinking to your team. It's smart to have a hunch about what kind of talent your team will need—but you won't get unexpected solutions with an expected team.

Write the names of your potential collaborators, partners, and team members here. Ensure you have a cross-generational and cross-functional team.

7. Determine Impact. (five minutes)

What impact will you make with your solution? How will you know your idea is making a difference? Is the impact you desire to make deep or wide? What are your measures of success? (Use this format: From X to Y by when?) If the project is successful what story will you be telling?

Describe your impact here.

8. Decide Next Steps. (five minutes)

Without the discipline to take action solutions remain ideas. What are the next steps needed to bring this solution to life? When you think of the initial steps ask the question, what needs to happen before that?

Describe the action steps here.

9. Present Your Idea to the Group. (ten minutes per team)

As part of this exercise each team will have five minutes to present its ideas and five minutes to answer questions from other group members.

In the real world you'd test your idea using a prototype or test group.

Questions: What did you learn? What worked? What did not? What adjustments need to be made? What impact did you have? What are your next steps?

Integrating the feedback you hear from the people you're designing for is one of the essential elements of human-centered design. You learned from people in the problem-understanding phase, and one of the best ways to keep learning from them is to show them what you've made and find out what they think.

Integrating feedback into your work and then coming up with another prototype is the best way to refine your idea until it's something that's bound to be impactful.

Describe your learning and next steps here.

Chapter 11

SEVEN MINDSETS AND ACTIONS TO CREATE YOUR OWN BLANK SLATE FOR CONGREGATIONAL AND COMMUNITY TRANSFORMATION

The previous chapter provided an opportunity to practice the process of human-centered design as a method for discovering innovative solutions.

Human-centered design is first about a mindset and then about taking action. These mindsets begin with deep empathy and continue towards innovative action to solve complex needs of people within communities.

Remember, the majority of Millennials and Gen Zers in neighborhoods throughout the United States do not attend any church. This sobering fact reminds us that there is a disconnect between churches and people. This speaks to a connectional, social, boundary-crossing relational need that must happen outside the church. It seeks to liberate individuals and communities from all forms of burden and oppression through the love of Jesus Christ.

This is the deeper, messier work of evangelism that is required to transform lives and communities.

We first encountered the work of human-centered design as pastors and church planters seeking to understand our community and determine how our churches could be a part of helping the neighborhood and church thrive. As church planters, during the prelaunch phase we surveyed the neighborhood using good old-fashioned paper surveys on clipboards at community events. We did weekly one-to-one conversations with community leaders. We visited local schools and listened to the needs of students, teachers, administrators and staff.

The data gathered shaped the core decisions, the DNA of the new church. For example, we originally offered Saturday night worship as an alternative to the traditional Sunday morning worship. Yet, after listening to the community and testing out the Saturday evening worship time, with only thirty-five people in attendance after three tries, we learned that if people were going to attend worship it would be on a Sunday morning beginning at 10:00 a.m. or 11:00 a.m., not Saturday night. This learning changed our course significantly and resulted in building a larger and more committed worshiping community. This is the heart of human-centered design. We listened and allowed the people we desired to reach to answer our questions.

Churches must continue to create new places of belonging for people in our neighborhoods. We must practice welcoming hospitality for people of all ages, economic status, races, and cultures. My prayer for church is that we will also be courageous enough to engage in kingdom building. May we be attentive as it bubbles up in our communities and bold enough to respond to the real needs of people. This is the heart of design thinking and the gospel of Jesus Christ.

A workshop on evangelism and outreach was recently facilitated with a group of thirty-four newly licensed United Methodist pastors. We discussed "who" and how they desired to reach new people within their ministry contexts. Almost all of the new pastors lamented that they wanted to reach younger and more diverse people but pastored congregations of people who were significantly older. This age gap between existing congregations and the community around them, reminds us of the urgent need to share the process of design thinking (more specifically, human-centered design) to create solutions that come from and resonate with the people we want to reach.

For any organization, embracing human-centered design means believing that all problems, even the seemingly impossible ones like poverty, violence, health care, housing, transportation sexism, racism, and education are solvable. It means believing that the people who face those problems every day are the ones who have the answer to solve them. It means problem-solvers from any sector have a method to design with communities, to deeply understand the people they're looking to serve, to brainstorm an unlimited number of ideas, and to create innovative new solutions rooted in people's actual needs and desired solutions. Here are seven essential mindsets for creating your own blank slate.

1. See Differently.

Jasmine loves to take pictures. Put a camera in her hand, and she is immediately in her happy place. When looking through the lens of a camera, she is invited to *see* things from a different perspective than she would ordinarily *see* them. Instead of rushing through a place or a situation, a photographer is observant—always looking for a story—always looking for what everyone else is missing.

A good photographer is merely looking to get a good enough shot—capture the moment as everyone else sees it. A great photographer is looking for what no one else sees—the best shot! No photographer can get the "best shot" without sacrifice. Photographers must risk looking crazy, getting in the way, maybe even coming across as a bit pushy or bossy to get the best shot.

As human-centered designers, we must live in a place of wonder—what are we missing because we're settling for a good shot and not looking for the best shot. What would we *see* if we stepped outside of our comfort zones? What would we *see* if we sacrificed our own wants for the desires of God in our lives, hearts, churches, and communities? What space might we make for others if we *see* what God *sees?* What might we be missing because we are looking with our natural eyes instead of through the lens of the Holy Spirit? Who or what is God trying to show us? How is God trying to shape us?

In the "love chapter" of the Bible, 1 Corinthians 13, *The Message* translation teaches us:

> We don't yet see things clearly. We're squinting in a fog, peering through a mist. But it won't be long before the weather clears and the sun shines bright! We'll see it all then, see it all as clearly as God sees us, knowing him directly just as he knows us! But for right now, until that completeness, we have three things to do to lead us toward that consummation: Trust steadily in God, hope unswervingly, love extravagantly. And the best of the three is love. (1 Corinthians 13:12-15 MSG)

Take some time to pray and to look around and see what you're missing. Ask God to give you a fresh perspective on situations in your life. Ask God to show you things the way that God sees them. Seek a fresh encounter with the Holy Spirit. Take the scenic route. Don't settle for a good enough shot. Ask God to give you eyes to see the best shot!

2. Let Go of the Outcome and Be Willing to Fail.

Lia served as the founding pastor of Renaissance UMC, a new church start, from 2010–2015 in Kansas City, Missouri. It was started in the building of a United Methodist church that closed after a sixty-year history. At its height in the 1960s it boasted over one thousand members. Beginning in the 1980s, membership declined as the neighborhood shifted from mostly white and middle-class to mostly African American and lower middle-class (with an average household income of $40,000). Renaissance launched in 2011. Eight years later, Renaissance is a second campus of St. James UMC in Kansas City; averages 100 people in Sunday worship; and continues to reach new people through its partnerships with the local school district, social service agencies, police department, and faith community. As a new church planter she did not know about the gathering of a launch team, outreach to a transitioning community, or rehabilitating a building with a rich history, or that deferred maintenance would be fruitful. She and the team had to let go of the outcome, be willing to fail, and trust that God would use their efforts toward good.

How often are you failing? What are you learning? Nelson Mandela is quoted as saying, "I never lose. I either win or I learn." Failure is an incredibly powerful tool for learning if we choose

109

to embrace it. In the work of church planting there is an average success rate of 50 percent. Yet, for every project that fails one succeeds, and for every experience there is great learning and people's lives are impacted. So, there is really no failure when our goal is learning and improving. Designing experiments, models, and encounters and then testing them is at the heart of blank slate design. So is an understanding that not all of them are going to work. As we seek to solve big problems, we're bound to fail. But if we adopt the right mindset, we'll inevitably learn something from that failure and have a better chance for success next time.

In an ironic pronouncement of outcomes in Matthew's Gospel, Jesus began to teach them. He said:

> Happy are people who are hopeless, because the kingdom of heaven is theirs. Happy are people who grieve, because they will be made glad. Happy are people who are humble, because they will inherit the earth. Happy are people who are hungry and thirsty for righteousness, because they will be fed until they are full. Happy are people who show mercy, because they will receive mercy. Happy are people who have pure hearts, because they will see God. Happy are people who make peace, because they will be called God's children. Happy are people whose lives are harassed because they are righteousness, because the kingdom of heaven is theirs. (Matthew 5:2-10 CEB)

This reminds us to *allow God's spirit to move us ahead* instead of always needing to *make* things happen. Admittedly, I'm not always good at this. Sometimes I'm a bit of a control freak and invest great energy into trying to plan, predict, and prevent things that I cannot perfectly plan, predict, or prevent. For me this action is about control, a fear of failure, and believing I know what's best. In a time of great uncertainty for the church and culture, there's no way to perfectly plan, predict, and prevent a way forward. Individually and collectively, we are called to trust that we're okay no matter what circumstances come our way. We don't need to micro-manage one another or the universe. We let go of the outcome. And we open ourselves to all sorts of wonderful possibilities that aren't there when we're attached to one "right" path.

What outcome is God calling you to let go of?

3. Decide That Innovation Is Mission-Critical.

Societies, class meetings, and bands are the hallmark of what has come to be known as the Methodist movement started by John Wesley. For some familiar with the movement these groups seem archaic. Yet, in eighteenth-century England and nineteenth-century America these innovations were radical. Bands, societies, and class meetings formed the root of a new way of life for Wesley's followers. As numbers grew he quickly saw he could not visit them all separately in their homes. So he told them, "If you will all...come together every Thursday, in the evening, I will gladly spend some time with you in prayer, and give you the best advice I can." Wesley comments:

> Thus arose, without any previous design on either side, what was afterwards called a Society—a very innocent name, and very common in London for any number of people associating themselves together.... They therefore united themselves "in order to pray together, to receive the word of exhortation, and to watch over one another in love, that they might help each other to work out their salvation." There is only one condition previously required in those who desire admission into this Society, "a desire to flee from the wrath to come, and to be saved from their sins."[1]

With a simple entrance requirement, the Methodist society was at once the easiest to seek and most demanding to be apart of.

Wesley responded to the needs of the people he served because he knew innovation was critical to the mission of holistic salvation.

The band meeting, an innovation patterned after the Moravians, consisted of a small group of either men or women gathered for encouragement, confession, and accountably. Wesley wrote:

> These therefore wanted some means of closer union; they wanted to pour out their hearts without reserve, particularly with regard to the sin which did still "easily beset" them, and the temptations which were most apt to prevail over them. And they were the more desirous of this when they observed, it was the express advice of an inspired writer, "Confess your faults one to another, and pray for one another, that ye may be healed." In compliance with their desire I divided them into smaller companies; putting the married or single men, and married or single women together.[2]

Again, Wesley innovated to meet the needs of people he was in constant and deep relationship with to form the bands. Wesley did not seek to change the Church of England's structure. Instead he innovated, or introduced something new, to meet needs that existed.

The class meeting was also an unexpected innovation. Wesley was increasingly concerned that many Methodists did not remain alive in the gospel. He wrote: "several grew cold, and gave way to the sins which had long easily beset them."[3] So, the societies were divided into "classes" of a dozen each. Leaders were appointed to secure weekly contributions toward the debt, and Wesley asked the leaders also to "make a particular inquiry into the behavior of those whom he saw weekly."[4] This provided the opportunity for exercising discipline. Importantly, the class meetings were not designed merely as growth groups or life groups in the way we think of them today. They didn't focus specifically on *fellowship*, although they certainly met some social need for community. The primary purpose was discipline in a life of discipleship.

This spring I (Lia) started participating in a band meeting with two other women. We realized that while we all attend different congregations on Sunday, we need community and accountability, which cannot be met in the context of a large gathering like a weekly worship service. Our band meeting conversations center around an understanding that sin is anything that separates us from God and one another. We use these questions to guide our conversations: What is aching your soul? What this week has nurtured your soul? Our conversations are a safe place for vulnerable sharing and mutual accountability. I am grateful for the presence of these special women of faith in my life.

Wesley's preaching in open fields, teaching holistic healing methods, and caring for the poor are also examples of his commitment to courageously try cutting-edge methods for the mission of holistic salvation without regard for the status quo.

Where are you afraid to break new ground? Who can experiment with you? When will you begin?

4. Practice Storytelling and Naming.

Storytelling is the speaking and hearing of one's experience while sharing a cup of coffee, sitting around a camp fire, singing songs, reciting poetry, preaching, sharing a book study with friends, and more. These stories are fabrics of our collective family, cultural, and religious history.[5] Everyone's story deserves to be told, especially those who have been systemically silenced, sidelined, and stereotyped. As the church leads more people to tell their stories, witness is made to the nexus, instead of separation of race, class, education, mental and physical ability, and religious identity. Through storytelling the naming of good and bad, justice and injustice, joy and pain, love and heartache are identified instead of ignored. As a result, the transformation of both individuals and society becomes possible and the mission of the church is lived out. Without stories, our connection with the depth of who we are is limited. Importantly, our stories of race, culture, gender, and other differences are gifts that illustrate the diversity of God.

Jasmine had been the first female, first African American, and youngest lead pastor of the historically Anglo Atlanta First United Methodist Church for just a few short months when Donald Trump, the forty-fifth President of the United States, was elected. Much of young and black America was in shock—reeling from the overt racism directed toward them in the wake of the election. Young black men, at alarming rates, were being gunned down by police officers. People with confederate flags in the back of their pick-up trucks were running people of color off of the roads in southern America. White people everywhere were saying, sharing, and doing harmful and detrimental things everywhere. Anyone who thought racism was a thing in the past was awakened to its current existence.

First Church was not used to the responsive political activist discourse that is central to the black church experience and to Jasmine's Christian upbringing. Pastor Jasmine had to address the situation from the pulpit because the historically Anglo congregation was now multi-cultural, multi-ethnic, and multi-generational. Pastor Jasmine had to address the situation because the gospel demands it.

Later that week, one of the Traditionalists in the church came by to see Pastor Jasmine. Angry at the "political talk" that came from the pulpit that Sunday, she admonished Pastor Jasmine that "we don't do that around here. I can't remember a time I've heard politics from this pulpit." But then the tenor of the conversation changed. The congregant said, "I just want to understand why you thought you needed to say that." Ah! Yes! Pastor Jasmine had been invited into a conversation—an opportunity to share a story.

Pastor Jasmine and the congregant spent the better part of an hour sharing about their upbringing in the very same city, generations and neighborhoods apart. Through sharing their stories, they gained a better understanding of each other and why it is important to talk politics from the pulpit in this day and age. Pastor Jasmine learned a new way to communicate with her new and diverse congregation. The congregant learned things about her hometown and people in it that she had no context for understanding. Storytelling turned the tide.

5. Be Relentless in Empathy and Belonging.

Renaissance is a campus of St. James UMC, an urban church in Kansas City, Missouri. As a community it's confronted with the realities of homelessness, joblessness, violence, drugs, teen pregnancy, and racism. The mission at the time of its founding was, "Helping people experience new life through Jesus Christ, thus making new disciples of Jesus Christ for the transformation of the world." This mission led the church to engage in diverse ministries, including a weekly community dinner, a summer sports camp for elementary school students, individual counseling, and a transformational Sunday worship experience. The church also engaged in discipleship with growth groups for adults, couples, youth, and children. These are examples of how the physical, mental, and spiritual needs of people in our neighborhoods are met in a context of community. These are spaces and places at St. James where people find belonging.

But, the overwhelming majority of people in neighborhoods throughout the United States do not attend any church. This disturbing fact reminds us that there is a deeper level of belonging that many churches are failing to facilitate. This type of belonging is a form of evangelism. It's a connectional, social, boundary-crossing evangelism, and it begins outside the church. It seeks to liberate individuals and communities from all forms of burden and oppression through the love of Jesus Christ. This is the deeper, messier work of evangelism that is required to transform our communities in the wake of unrest in communities such as Ferguson, Missouri, a few miles from where Lia grew up in St. Louis. This liberating work can be done in partnership with a variety of organizations and agencies, but authentic spiritual liberation is the primary responsibility of the church of Jesus Christ. It starts in the street, engages with local leaders in law enforcement, local government, and school districts, and includes local congregations. This may not immediately build the church's worship attendance, small group participation, or financial offerings, but it's the work of kingdom building and is essential to fulfill our mission of transforming the world.

The foundation for this work is empathy. Empathy is the capacity to walk a mile in other people's shoes; to understand their lives; to experience their feelings, thoughts, or attitudes; and to start solving problems from their perspective. Importantly, empathy (which is not the same as sympathy) is practiced from afar as we often say "you're in my thoughts and prayers." Empathy is demonstrated by presence in the mist of everyday life with one another.

Who is God calling you toward in empathy?

6. Practice the Work of Empowerment.

A way of demonstrating empathy is empowerment. A typical understanding of power is having the ability or resources to accomplish a goal. When power is able to be exercised individually or collectively it produces the feelings vitality and freedom. Empowerment is "the process by which individuals, families, groups and communities increase their personal, interpersonal, socioeconomic, and political strength and influence in order to improve their well being."[6] Empowerment is not granted from an external source. It emerges from within as persons and communities acknowledge and appreciate the gifts and responsibilities that come from our collective physical, emotional, mental, and spiritual depths. Power is multifaceted and evidenced in diverse and interrelated ways (power over, power in, power with). As a result, innovation requires analyzing and deconstructing power relationships to ensure women and men, children and adults across ethnicities, cultures, and economic status have access to resources and abilities to achieve individual and collective goals.

The church is called to be a place of empathy, empowerment, and belonging for people in our neighborhoods. We must lead the way in the practices of welcoming hospitality, radical inclusion, and bold justice. My prayer for the church is that we will be courageous and attentive as needs bubble up in our communities, that we will be bold and encourage this kingdom force to spread, and that our local congregations would be transformed. We all belong to Christ, and in Christ we find our place of belonging through hospitality, empathy, and empowerment.[7]

Who are you being called to empower and create spaces of belonging with? What's stopping you? What's the easiest step you can take today towards this person(s)?

7. Imagine, Hope, and Act.

If you could create anything for your future in the next year, what is it that you'd like to create for your life, your church, or community? We've asked this question hundreds of times as coachesand workshop facilitators. This is a question of imagination, vision, and optimism toward our dreams. This question sets the foundation for taking on a big challenge, especially one as large and complex as the social ills of poverty, education, health, and spiritual healing. It's a mindset of hopefulness and confidence about desired outcomes. We have to believe that progress is a realistic option. If we didn't, we wouldn't even try. It is the belief of possibility, the idea that even if we don't know the answer, that it's out there and that we can find it collectively. And, while we know there will be challenges along the way, committing to finding a way to creatively use the resources available, overcome obstacles and make progress is essential to the work of transformation.

Foundational to a mindset of imagination, envisioning, and hopefulness is faith. A definition of faith that resonates with us is, "A life orientation of the whole person in partnership with God."[8] This is not a generic faith that lives afar and avoids messiness. It is an active faith that's activated in the context of particular communities amidst their hopes and struggles with God. This is not an individual faith only concerned with personal salvation and the afterlife. It is faith in community, in partnership, with one another and God.

In the New Testament, a word frequently used for sharing with someone in a common bond is *koinonia*. *Koinonia* describes a life in partnership or communion with one another as described in 1 Corinthians 10:16-17, "Is not the cup of thanksgiving for which we give thanks a participation in the blood of Christ? And is not the bread that we break a participation in the body of Christ? Because there is one loaf, we, who are many, are one body, for we all share the one loaf."[9] In these relationships we choose to participate in celebration and struggle together, and in time realize we are set free for one another. In this place trust is built and the gift of partnership can be realized.[10]

A Historical Case Study: Education and Emancipation

An example of *koinonia* is demonstrated by the active faith of churches, both black and white, in the education of freed slaves in the US South after the Civil War from 1865 to the early 1900s.

In 1865 when the Civil War ended and the US government passed the Fourteenth Amendment declaring slavery illegal. At least theoretically, the doors of freedom and opportunity were open for enslaved blacks in the South. Subsequently, four million African Americans faced the task of reconstructing their lives and charting a future of freedom. At the center of these reconstruction efforts was the church, both black and white, with a primary task of educating slaves in literacy. "Despite the fact that teaching a slave to read and write was illegal during slavery, one of the most persistent desires of

119

the slaves was to be educated. No other area of black life received a higher priority from black churches than education."[11] The slaves who learned to read and write were empowered to interpret biblical scriptures, to teach others, and to prove to whites that they were capable of learning and understanding God's word. In fact, Sunday schools were often the places where blacks began their education as they listened, remembered, and read scriptures.[12]

Education, according to the *Dictionary of Afro-American Slavery*, is "a process of cultural transmission and transformation."[13] In contrast, most studies of North American slavery define education in terms of literacy training in formal schools, informal tutoring, or self-teaching, but prior to 1865 the primary training slaves received was vocational, or on-the-job training.[14] Imagine a fictional, yet realistic, twelve-year-old girl born in 1810 into slavery in Charleston, South Carolina, named Louise. She receives no formal education for the first ten years of her life, but elders teach her from infancy about her culture and how to survive in slavery. Louise has many friends among the slave children and acquaintances among the master's children as she carries their books to school. Louise knows the value of community for survival. While Emancipation, and the scattering of slaves after the Civil War, provided freedom it also ended vocational and cultural education in this unique form.[15]

When the Civil War ended, Protestant Churches from the North launched crusades to bring literacy to four million newly-freed slaves.[16] White missionary societies such as the American Mission Society (A.M.A.), the American Baptist Home Mission Society (A.B.H.M.S.), the Quakers, and individual white donors all helped to establish black schools in the South, many of which began in the basements of African American churches. In 1865, the Freedman's Bureau was also founded by the US Congress to work with religious and charitable organizations to establish schools for blacks. "By 1870, the Freedman's Bureau operated over 2,600 schools in the South with 3,300 teachers educating 150,000 students."[17]

Henry H. Mitchell, an African American historian, reports that the A.M.A. was "unequaled in the founding of schools of quality."[18] This quality was built upon well-educated and devoted teachers, both black and white.

Other predominately white denominations that founded schools in the South included Methodists, Presbyterians, Episcopalians, and Lutherans. The Methodist Church North founded many secondary schools and eight colleges in the South. One such school was Walden University in 1865 (its health science professional school is known today as Meharry Medical College).[19] Other schools founded by the Methodist Church North include Clark Atlanta University in Atlanta, Georgia; Wiley College in Marshall, Texas; and Bennett College in Greensboro, North Carolina. Presbyterians, Episcopalians, and Lutherans, although they did not take strong stands against slavery, founded dozens of black colleges. For example, in 1854 Ashman Institute (later Lincoln University) was founded in Chester County, Pennsylvania, near Philadelphia, by the Presbyterians. "It was the first institution for the higher education of African American men in the United States (it did not become coed until the 1950s)."[20]

"The black church also placed a high value on education and Baptists, Methodists, and Pentecostals established their own colleges and seminaries."[21] Beyond education in reading, writing, and mathematics black schools emphasized religious and moral education to strengthen the black race. Many believed that cultural development of young minds was just as important as traditional education.

The African Methodist Episcopal (A.M.E), African Methodist Episcopal Zion (A.M.E.Z.), and the Colored Methodist Episcopal (C.M.E.) denominations as well as the African American Baptists launched dozens of primary and secondary schools from 1867–1919, often in small rural communities. Using African American teachers, who were certified, black churches launched their own schools. Church-based schools allowed many black children to receive an education who did not have access to white-sponsored schools. Henry H. Mitchell writes, "Even now a highly disproportionate number of the leaders in African American communities are graduates of such church-sponsored schools."[22]

The Methodist Church was particularly supportive of educational institutions because of the social class of many of its members and their requirements for clergy ordination. Traditionally, many black Methodists, while poor compared to whites, were considered middle-income blacks or strived to become middle-class. Consequently, they stressed education and an educated clergy through their connectional polity. For example, Bishop Daniel Payne of the A.M.E. Church, who had been a schoolmaster in Baltimore, set high educational standards for the denomination by insisting upon formal training for its ministers. He also encouraged churches to organize schools in their communities as an aspect of their ministry. Bishop Payne was also the driving force behind the establishment of Wilberforce University in 1856, the first institution of higher learning founded by African Americans in the United States.[23]

The black church, since its beginnings, has embraced its responsibility to "be involved in the total liberation of black personhood and to help empower the black community."[24] It advanced a "black theology of liberation" long before the phrase was popularized by James Cone and others. God was black for African Americans, because it reminded the people that God's interaction with them was personal and communal.[25] God enabled an oppressed people to take control of their destiny through education and to live free and purposeful lives. People of all denominations, races, classes, and experiences supported the education and socialization of blacks in schools and society. This example of *koinonia* is demonstrated by the active faith of churches, both black and white. This should inspire us today toward imagination, envisioning, hopefulness, and an active faith.

When is the last time that you attempted something so big, that without God, it was bound to fail? What if today became that day? When starting with a blank slate, transformation is possible.

Section 5

TOPICS FOR FURTHER THINKING

In this section we'll share three important topics for further thinking given the increasing cultural diversity in the United States and around the world. We've included this section because effective leadership today and into the twenty-second century requires a deeper understanding of gender, racial, economic, and lifestyle diversity more than ever before. No longer will broad generalizations about people different from us suffice. The United States and the world are already (not becoming) diverse in lifestyle and culture. As of 2017, "Forty-seven states and 90 percent of the counties have an absolute decline in white population under age 20. All net growth of children in this country is coming from racial and ethnic minorities."[1] Additionally, with the broad access to the Internet and cell phones, individuals increasingly expect products, services, and experiences immediately to meet their needs and make their lives better. When an experience does not deliver upon these expectations, people (yes consumers) will explore other options. Gone are the days of limited choices and settling for what's available.

As a result, spiritual leaders must connect the stated and unstated needs and desires of individual people and tribes to the "real presence of Christ...if they are to become conduits of Grace."[2] In his book, *Spiritual Leadership: Why Leaders Lead and Who Seekers Seek to Follow*, Tom Bandy names eight existential anxieties that are addressed by eight experiences of Christ led by eight types of spiritual leaders with different experiences and expectations.

125

Within each of these categories there are many nuances based on culture. No longer is there a monolithic identity of people by age, ethnicity, wealth, education, geography, nor family status. Customized experiences are no longer an exception, they are an expectation, even in the church.

A recent global report cites, "Cultural diversity has emerged as a key concern at the turn of a new century. Yet the meanings attached to this catch-all term are as varied as they are shifting."[3] Some see cultural diversity within a church and community as a positive, enabling deeper understanding, relationships, and impact. For others, cultural differences are misunderstood, feared, and cause many conflicts. This second diagnosis is too often the reality within some churches. So an essential challenge for leaders is to lead the way and to propose a vision of cultural diversity and thereby to clarify how differences in gender, race, economics and lifestyle are strengths to the church and world—rather than those differences being a threat to the status quo.

Chapter 12

INTERFAITH AND INTERGENERATIONAL DIALOGUE: REACHING IN LOVE AND LIBERATION

A t a recent community workshop Lia reconnected with a young woman, a Millennial, from a previous church she pastored. The woman shared that, while she was still a member of the church, she no longer actively attended because the church lacked inclusivity. She lamented that she has Jewish, Muslim, and atheist friends and cannot accept that Jesus is the only way to connect with God and have everlasting life. She believes that all faiths should include acceptance, love, and a willingness to live and learn with others. It is the content of a person's character and the intent of his or her heart that one should value. She advocated that race, experience, gender, faith, and other differences are gifts that illustrate the diversity of God. This describes what some scholars name "a new religious consciousness."[1] Catholic-Hindu scholar Ramon Panikkar writes in his article titled "The Unknown Christ":

> [T]he encounter of traditions through multi-faith (and multi-cultural) dialogue is crucial in the new situation of radical pluralism that confronts our world because no single religion, culture,

127

or tradition holds a universal solution for either our theoretical or our practical human problems...no more will one religion, culture, or tradition impose itself on peoples of diverse and less powerful traditions.[2]

Since the post-Enlightenment period in Europe and North America (roughly 1687), there has been a tendency to devalue cultural diversity in favor of universal truths. For example, feminist theologian Karen Baker-Fletcher writes, "Women, nature, and people of color have been cast low in the hierarchy. In dichotomous dualisms, whiteness has been viewed as morally, ontologically, and aesthetically superior to blackness or color, male to female, heterosexual to homosexual, culture to nature, upper-class to lower class, etc."[3] Likewise, individual or personal expressions of salvation and Christology, privileging intellectualism, and dualistic views of secular and sacred worlds are characteristics of modernity.[4] In contrast, Panikkar argues, "If we privatize and individualize Christ, how will we break through the veil of fear and distrust that shields us from other religions?"[5] In other words, Panikkar is challenging Christians to a greater vision of Christ that is more inclusive. We interpret this as a call to unity, caring, and conversation among people of diverse faith traditions and understandings of the person and work of Jesus Christ.

In today's context, this call challenges Christians to believe in the revelation of God in Jesus, while also believing that we "do not have a monopoly on the knowledge of Christ."[6] In other words, the revelation of God in Christ is greater than just Jesus and can be seen in all humanity. Another response to pluralism has been to assert that all religious people who follow the teachings of Jesus, such as loving God and neighbor, are Christian whether they self-identify as Christian or not.[7] This understanding keeps

Christianity as superior and at the center of all religions. In contrast, many feminist theologians have sought to seek commonalities and multiple truths across religions, cultures, and values to fight moral and ethical issues such as gender bias, racism, and classism.

Still, the question, "How does one receive salvation without a known belief in the incarnation of Jesus Christ?" may linger in your mind as you contemplate these approaches. Some answers to these questions lie in what Panikkar calls "the divine life of the Trinity, who, marked by a consummate union in love, will pervade everything at the end of time."[8] In other words, to value the mystery of Christ through diversity in religion, race, class, gender, and other differences is to reject notions of hierarchy and supremacy and to embrace unity, mutuality, and love. Salvation then consists in reaching for our own fullness, in sharing the divine nature of God.

So how can the multicultural, multigenerational ministry of the local church reflect the universal Christ? One way is through interfaith dialogue. The process of conversation across faiths includes intentional listening and learning from one another. A strength of this approach is that its primary purpose is to learn, not to convert one another to their faith. This model challenges us to consider the last time we have had a conversation with the poor, oppressed, abused, addicted, and non-Christian of our communities. Unfortunately, this type of dialogue has been sorely lacking in many of our local churches. Going forward we believe interfaith dialogue is crucial to the life and ministry of the worldwide community of all God's people.

We envision women gathering for intergenerational and interfaith dialogue. For example, our dialogue could begin by focusing on common concerns of life for children and families such as education, parenting, health care, and spiritual nurturing. It could then blossom to include actions such as after-school tutoring of children, working in women's shelters, and advocating for justice against all kinds of class, race, culture, and religious oppression. Additionally, we imagine the sharing of spiritual practices and theology, Scripture studies, short-term topical studies, and small groups that apply faith to particular life challenges. For example, a series called "Faith Talk" could include monthly meetings with a focus on expanding the knowledge of commonalities and uniqueness across religions. A five-step process for interfaith meeting, as adapted from *The Faith Club*[9] could include topics and questions such as the following.

Examine Your Religion—What religion are you and why? How do your religious background and practices influence your life and beliefs?

Put Your Stereotypes on the Table—What stereotypes do you hold of anyone of another faith or denomination? How do you stereotype members of your own faith?

Define Your God—Do you believe God exists? What is God? How do you feel about people who don't believe in God? What is heaven? What is universal about the way we experience God? What is unique?

Explore Prayer and Holy Text—Do you pray? What is prayer? What role does prayer and scripture play in your faith? What questions do you have about prayers, scriptures, and rituals of other faiths?

Think About Religion on the World Stage—How does religion affect how we view the world? How does religion contribute to world conflict? Does it ever foster peace?

Inherent in this model of interfaith dialogue is an element of *koinonia* or "partnership, participation, communion, community."[10] It is a way of reaching out to the "other" in love and liberation. It is sharing and giving, enabled by the spirit of Christ that, as Ilia Delio writes, "Is a way of coming to understand a fuller, richer expression of humanity within the unfolding diversity of creation."[11] It describes lavish sharing, sacrifice, and giving in service to God and neighbor through our common bond of a multicultural, multigenerational Christ.

Questions for Reflection

1. What do you appreciate most about interfaith and multi-generational conversations?

2. What challenges you most about interfaith and multigenerational relationships?

3. Sociologist and theologian Adair T. Lummis writes, "Internationally, religious pluralism can negatively evoke bigotry against a whole people whose leaders are at odds with another's."[12] How can leaders promote understanding between political leaders and people around the world through

dialogue despite the diversity of experiences, religious doctrines, and practices?

4. Women across many religions have come together to denounce patriarchy in their traditions and advocate for ecumenical religious pluralism. How do women decide when to exit patriarchal religions and join other communities of faith or to stay within religions and advocate for transformation?

Chapter 13

UBUNTU: A DIVINE ASSIGNMENT FOR MULTICULTURAL AND INTERGENERATIONAL MISSION

Ubuntu is a word that comes from the Zulu ethnic group in South Africa and it describes the essence of being human.[1] It is an African philosophy of community, interconnectedness, mutual respect, solidarity, and caring of humanity and serves as the spiritual foundation of many African societies.[2] South African professor Dirk J. Louw writes, "It both describes human being as 'being-with-others' and prescribes what 'being-with-others' should be all about."[3] In other words, being fully human is only possible when we are in relationship with a community of people. Louw emphasizes that the context of ubuntu in African culture is both secular and religious and is a model of life and a way of looking at the world.[4]

Ubuntu describes an essential of the intergenerational and multicultural Christian mission. It puts anyone who is oppressed at the center of mission. Mission, from the Latin word *misso,* is "to be sent."[5] *Misso Dei* means to be sent by God on a divine task into the world.[6] In other words, mission is to serve God through serving others, especially the oppressed. *Apostle*, from the Greek word *apostolos*, is "one who is sent on the authority of another."[7] Combining the concepts of ubuntu, mission, and apostle, my definition of mission in an intergenerational and multicultural context is a *divine assignment by God and for God to be in solidarity with the world, especially the oppressed, or ubuntu.* Ultimately, God through the life and work of Christ and by the power of the Holy Spirit enables the full humanity of all people and the fullness of creation thorough mission. This chapter will recommend five marks of multicultural and multigenerational mission and recommend how to apply the marks of mission to a local church using experience in conversation with biblical scripture, history, culture, and Methodist Theology.

The primary text for the marks of mission is Luke 4:18-19 as inspired by Isaiah's prophesy:

> The Spirit of the Lord is upon me, because the Lord has anointed me. He has sent me to preach good news to the poor, to proclaim release to the prisoners and recovery of sight to the blind, to liberate the oppressed, and to proclaim the year of the Lord's favor.

Five Marks of Mission for an Intergenerational and Multicultural Church

1. Bring good news to the poor.
2. Proclaim release to the captives.
3. Proclaim recovery of sight to the blind.
4. Let the oppressed go free.
5. Proclaim the year of the Lord's favor.

1. Bring Good News to the Poor.

Jesus began his earthly ministry proclaiming fulfillment of God's prophesy in the scroll of Isaiah and thus bringing good news to the poor. To begin our discussion of Jesus's ministry and the call to mission we must define who is Jesus in this context, who are the poor, and what is good news. Jesus as prophet and servant speaks in the text who, by the anointing of the Holy Spirit, speaks on behalf of God. The mission of Jesus, and thus followers of Jesus, is to bring good news to the poor. Good news is the presence of Christ in the lives of individuals and in situations of suffering and oppression in the community. Second, good news is the death and resurrection of Jesus Christ assuring the possibility of freedom from oppression today and eternally. Finally, the good news is "liberty that gives the believer an unlimited sense of freedom to live according to the spirit of Christ independent of external custom or constraint."[8] In other words, good news gives Christ-followers the authority to reject all people and systems that diminish human life. Importantly, the good news is not simply a future spiritual hope it is also a present possibility for followers of Jesus Christ.[9]

The poor in this text are people and communities who are economically disadvantaged, spiritually impoverished, and socially outcast. Often the poor within communities are also marginalized or "destitute and disadvantaged people in a wealthy environment."[10] For example, poor black women and thus black families are often the poorest, most destitute, and most disadvantaged economically in systems of patriarchy where white men and their families are the most powerful and wealthy. To take this a step further, a poor black lesbian woman would be socially outcast even more. Dr. Maulana Karenga, founder of Kwanzaa, a celebration of African and African American self-determination and culture, shares this vision of economic justice:

> In a world where greed, resource seizure, and plunder have been globalized with maximum technological and military power, we must uphold the principle and practice of *Ujamaa* (Cooperative Economics) or shared work and wealth. This principle reaffirms the right to control and benefit from the resources of one's own lands and to an equitable and just share of the goods of the world.[11]

In other words, the mission of spreading good news to the poor is inclusive of practical help such as improved personal finances and jobs for black families. In the context of the local church, here are three practical ways to bring good news (the love of Christ) to the poor in the black community as adapted from pastor and practical theologian Michael L. Cook.[12]

1. Develop an economic development ministry that helps to promote home ownership, savings, investments, and entrepreneurship.

2. Form partnerships with existing organizations like HUD Homes, Habitat for Humanity, and FHA to encourage homeownership.

3. Establish a credit union at church to provide low-interest or no-interest loans to start small businesses, short-term investments, invest in real estate, and so on.

These are just a few practical ways to empower people in struggling financial situations beyond (not in lieu of) the typical ministries of free meals and clothes. Indeed, there are many ways to bring good news to the oppressed poor in society when there is a desire from the heart to do so.

2. Proclaim Release to the Captives.

A second mark of mission is the proclamation and work of releasing captives. Release in this text is from the Greek word *aphesis*. "*Aphesis* appears in the Leviticus 25:10 as the translation of the Hebrew for *jubilee* and identified the 'release' as being that of debtors during a jubilee year. But Luke also uses *aphesis* for *forgiveness* in 24:47."[13] In other words, release can be physical, spiritual, or social liberation.

Captives are also people bound physically, spiritually, or socially. Some may be imprisoned unfairly for their faith. Others may desire spiritual forgiveness and release from the emotional guilt of sin. In the black community today (due in part to systems of racism and patriarchy), captives include black men who are interrogated, arrested, and imprisoned at unjust rates. Black women are captives in systems of subordination in church and society due to their race and gender. Historically, black women also have been bound by sexual exploitation as their bodies have been abused as the property of another since the inception of chattel slavery. Additionally, captives include those enslaved by drugs, alcohol, sexual addictions, and so on. Proclaiming the good news in situations of physical, emotional, and social hostage must not be an add-on in the black community. It is critical for the liberation of individuals, communities, and nations. In the context of the local church, here are two practical ways to release the captives in the black community as adapted from Dr. Sherrill McMillian, medical doctor and church member:

1. Confront the silence and talk about issues of physical, sexual, and mental abuse in black families. Develop a free Christian counseling ministry for church and community members along with small covenant groups to connect people with common challenges.

2. Preach and teach from the pulpit on silent concerns such as abuse, mental illness, incarceration, and sexuality. Collaborate with community agencies to offer support groups, reentry programs, and health screenings for church and community members.

3. Offer community workshops on the topics above for churches and schools.[14]

These are a few practical ways to empower people to live beyond physical, mental, spiritual, and social captivity. Through preaching, counseling, teaching, and loving people we proclaim the God-desired release from bondage for all who are captive.

3. Proclaim Recovery of Sight to the Blind.

A third mark of mission is the proclamation and work of the recovery of sight by the blind. This means more than the restoration of physical sight to those who are blind or even healing to the sick. Jesus proclaims a spiritual awakening so people will know him as the true Messiah, repent of their sins, and heal relationships. African theologian Samuel O. Abogunrin writes:

> The Apostle Paul explained to King Agrippa the purpose of his call and mission to both the Jews and Gentiles thus: "To open their eyes that they may turn from darkness to light and from the power of Satan to God, that they may receive the forgiveness *(aphesis)* of sin and a place among those who are sanctified by faith in me" (Acts 26:17-18).[15]

The mission of recovery of sight is the spiritual baptism and ongoing communion of individuals, communities, and even political kingdoms. This work is not by physical force, but by God's spiritual power, love, and grace. Jesus's message left many

Jews disillusioned because he was not the "radical political leader, leading a military uprising against Rome as they anticipated."[16] Likewise, today people may not realize their need for spiritual revitalization and communion with God. As a result, inherent in this mark mission is unity between people of diverse ages, races, genders, classes, and cultures. The African principle of *Umoja* (unity) describes this mission. Dr. Maulana Karenga writes:

> *Umoja* (Unity) invites us to an alternative sense of solidarity, a peaceful togetherness as families, communities and fellow human beings. It teaches us the oneness of our people, everywhere, the common ground of our humanity with others and our shared status as possessors of dignity and divinity. However, it also encourages us to feel at one with and in the world, to be constantly concerned about its health and wholeness, especially as we face the possibility of climate change and other disasters around the world.[17]

In the context of the local church, here are two practical ways toward spiritual transformation and unity in the black community as adapted from Johnny B. Hill, PhD.[18]

1. Uplift biblical images of family (including the Trinity) and demonstrate the importance of empowering relationships within the church and community. For example, opportunities should be given for people to serve in leadership positions who have been marginalized by age, race, gender, class, length of church membership, and so on. Partnerships with community agencies and schools are also important to demonstrate how to live in communion with others.

2. Offer a holistic ministry of Christian Education that goes beyond Bible study to include theological and practical discussions about life issues affecting the community such as home foreclosure, unemployment, drug abuse, single parenting, and so on.

4. Let the Oppressed Go Free.

A fourth mark of mission is the proclamation and actuality of freedom in mind, body, and spirit for the oppressed. Through Jesus Christ, individuals and communities can experience independence and creativity instead of domination and exploitation by people and systems in power. For example, Abogunrin writes:

> Freedom is not without its own obligations in that it implies an uncoerced response from those to whom it is offered. People have to decide whether they want to be free. Freedom has to be appropriated, by willingly accepting the freedom offered in Christ. Freedom in Christ is total because it affects the whole person, and their situation. Freedom is what one experiences, in the spiritual, moral, social, emotional, economic and political spheres of life. It is simply an inner feeling of freedom from the bondage of sin. The total freedom is present in and is at work in the way people who live in a community or nation structure their lives together.

In other words, the church is called to the Kwanzaa principle and practice of Kuumba (creativity) in the ways we heal, repair, rebuild, and renew the world and relationships. In the black community, single black women head the majority of households and represent the majority of church membership. In contrast, "more than one million black men are in prison or jail or on parole. That's a million fathers, sons, grandsons, brothers, and uncles locked up and locked down—mostly the result of a lack of decent jobs in the urban centers since factories shut down in the early seventies and manufacturing shifted towards globalization."[19] Despite this grim reality, there is hope through Jesus Christ for freedom from oppression and for black males to become strong, caring fathers of faith. In the context of the local church, here is one practical way toward the mission of freedom and partnership in the black community as adapted from Johnny B. Hill, PhD.

> Participate in the development of African American boys' identity, purpose and gifts, through mentoring programs. This program must be led in partnership with men in the church and community. As boys see what it means to be a father, son, friend, and so on, who practices his faith in Jesus Christ boys are more likely emulate them as role models. Within mentoring relationships, open dialogue is also critical to encourage boys to discuss important topics such as sexuality, relationships, family, and so on.

5. Proclaim the Year of the Lord's Favor.

The fifth mark of mission is the holistic proclamation and actuality that, in Jesus, God assures salvation today, immediately, for believers and forever more. "Today is an important word for Luke. It occurs 12 times in Luke and only 9 times in the other three gospels combined. For Luke today is a moment of radical change."[20] In other words, God's salvation and transforming presence is with us today through the incarnation of Jesus Christ and the sending of the Holy Spirit. Today there is hope, peace, patience, kindness, opportunity, and equal rights through Jesus Christ.

Today the African American community is experiencing the best and worst of times. The first African American president of the United States, elected in 2008, represents unprecedented achievement by some blacks, yet enslavement still exists for African Americans fifty years after the civil rights movement of the 1960s enabled integration of schools, corporations, and neighborhoods. Enslavement takes place in inner cities of America as well as the suburbs where the black middle-class has migrated. In the PBS special "The Two Nations of Black America," five characteristics emerged that define blacks in the inner cities of America: (1) single female head of household, (2) welfare dependent, (3) marginally educated (high school or less), (4) chronically unemployed, and (5) criminal recidivism (in and out of jail).[21] These ills are a result of oppression and can only be cured when blacks and whites, young and old, poor and rich, Christian and non-Christian work together through the liberating love of Jesus Christ to loose the chains oppression.

Our definition of mission in a multicultural, intergenerational context is a *divine assignment by God and for God to be in solidarity with the world, especially the oppressed, or ubuntu.* Ubuntu is lived out through five marks of mission of liberation based on Luke 4:18-19. For leaders of mission in the body of Christ the critical skill for success is what Walter Brueggemann describes in Donald E. Messer's book *Contemporary Images of Christian Ministry* as "the prophetic imagination"[22] or an alternative consciousness. Our challenge is to stand within the culture but to transform it by the leading and power of the Holy Spirit toward justice, equality, and freedom. This is not simply a matter of addressing specific social issues, but imagining and proclaiming a vision of a reconstructed society informed by the best of afro-centric and Christian values. To do this we must understand our collective experience, history, and culture because theology cannot be separated from the community that it represents. It assumes that truth has been given to the community at the moment of its birth.[23] Our missiology must also be biblical theology because the Bible is a source that proclaims that God is a God of liberation, who speaks to the oppressed and abused, and assures us that divine righteousness will vindicate suffering. May we live and proclaim new life in Christ as people liberated, loved, and empowered by God.

Questions for Reflection

1. What do you appreciate most about interfaith and multi-generational mission?

2. What challenges you most about interfaith and multigenerational mission?

3. Using a blank slate, contextual, design-centered model, how can your congregation uniquely:

   Bring good news to the poor?

Proclaim release to the captives?

Proclaim recovery of sight to the blind?

Let the oppressed go free?

Proclaim the year of the Lord's favor?

INTERGENERATIONAL AND MULTICULTURAL ATONEMENT, RECONCILIATION, AND PEACE

Hurricane Maria formed in the Atlantic Ocean, first reaching hurricane status on September 17, 2017, and elevating to a category five status one day later, devastated the Caribbean island nation of Dominica and then Puerto Rico with winds topping 160 miles per hour. It is the strongest hurricane on record to make landfall in this area.[1] The destruction of human life, property, and the spirit of its people cannot be underestimated. Many wonder if these islands can rebuild their infrastructure and restore hope to their people after an emergency unparalleled in the history of the Caribbean. In the wake of destruction like in Puerto Rico, an unincorporated territory of the United States, can atonement affect the people and give them hope? Can a renewed relationship with God facilitate the healing of a people? Is reconciliation a way forward? This chapter will provide an understanding of atonement and reconciliation by scholars Thomas F. Torrance, Donald K. McKim, Eugene Teselle, Delores S. Williams, and Lucy Tatman and inform our "blank slate" conversation for ministry today and into the twenty-second century.

Thomas F. Torrance in his text, *Atonement: The Person and Work of Christ*, defines "at-one-ment"[2] as the creation of a new personal relationship between God and humanity or reconciliation.[3] In other words, a new bond, connection, union, or attachment is created between humanity and God. This union between God and humanity is a two-way street as God reaches out to humanity and humanity reaches back to God. This bond is at the soul, heart, core, or spirit of who we are as humanity. We are persons created to be in union with God.

Eugene Teselle, Professor of Church History and Theology, defines "at-one-ment as the reconciliation of sinners with God, especially through the cross, as communicated through the gospel and the sacraments."[4] Both Torrance's and Teselle's definitions emphasize God's initiative to reconcile relationships through the Jesus. They also accentuate the need for a human response to God's initiation. A distinction in Teselle's definition is his emphasis on the means of grace such as baptism and Holy Communion. Teselle emphasizes how God "empowers humanity to a new mode of life"[5] while Torrance emphasizes God's action significantly more than humanity's response. Similar to Torrance and Teselle, Donald K. McKim in *Westminster Dictionary of Theological Terms*[6] defines atonement as affecting salvation by the reestablishing of a relationship between God and humanity or being "at one" through the death of Jesus Christ on the cross.[7] McKim, similar to Torrance, emphasizes God's action through Jesus Christ versus humanity's response.

In contrast to Torrance, Teselle, and McKim womanist scholars such as Delores William debate the need for Christian atonement theories based on Jesus dying on the cross. Delores S. Williams provides a critique of atonement theory from the perspective of African American women's oppression in the context of social-role surrogacy. Williams questions if the image of Jesus on the cross standing in the role of a sinful humanity is "coerced surrogacy."[8] If so, she believes it supports humanity, black women in particular, being today's surrogate or substitute to do things other women and men find undesirable. As an alternative to atonement through surrogacy and the cross, Williams suggests that it is "Jesus' life of resistance and by survival strategies he used to help people survive the death of identity"[9] that is salvific for humanity. This understanding affirms Jesus's life and ministry instead of his blood on the cross. Womanist atonement theories like Williams's are rooted in the experience of black women and affirms life, freedom, and joy for all of humanity in lieu of suffering. Notably, this understanding of atonement also differs from Torrance's by starting with women's experience instead of scripture.

Feminist scholars such as Linda J. Vogel understand reconciliation as "a way of being in relationship that links salvation and healing; it encompasses the whole creation."[10] In other words, God so loved the world that God enables all people rich and poor, female and male, from east to west to journey in and toward the "kindom (kingdom) of God."[11] This kingdom is one of peace, justice, love, forgiveness, inclusiveness, and calmness with God and humanity. Feminist scholars such as Catherine LaCugna advocate that it is "our relationship to others, which is indistinguishable from our relationship to Jesus Christ that determines whether we are or not finally incorporated in to God's household."[12] Similar to womanist theologians, feminists focus on women's experiences and empowering women through reconciliation with God.

Importantly, God's atonement is more than just an impersonal exchange. It is a personal relationship that is restored where God forgives and cancels out sin, shows favor to humanity for God's purposes, and the renewal of the very essence of humanity happens by God's grace. Reconciliation is also a profound and radical act on God's part. It is a radical act of love that makes each of us a child of God in sacraments such as baptism and offers forgiveness in Holy Communion. It symbolizes the old is terminated and there is a new beginning in Christ for all of creation, human and nonhuman, which is being reunited to God in peace.[13] People of every race, culture, sex, and religion are being reconciled to God. Even our enemies are being reconciled to God.

These varied definitions atonement and reconciliation by Torrance, McKim, Teselle, Williams, and Vogel ultimately call all of humanity and the church to forgiveness and reconciliation on behalf of the world. We start by listening to all voices and speaking in the voice and context of the people. By understanding people we can hear the unlikely bearers of God's word in our mist such as Puerto Ricans and Americans, women and children, immigrants and natives. We must stretch to be a symbol of God's love and bearers of peace to our friends, neighbors, and even enemies. By God's grace, may our table of reconciliation be a place of healing and hope for all.

Questions for Reflection

1. What do you appreciate most about these theologies of atonement and reconciliation?

2. What challenges you most about atonement and reconciliation?

3. Reconciliation is experienced between God and humanity, individuals and between groups. Can one type of reconciliation be experienced alone or are they interrelated somehow? Can an individual truly be at peace with God and not with our neighbors?

4. What lessons gleaned from this chapter are most important for the church today? How is atonement and reconciliation practiced within your church and community?

CONCLUSION

In this book we aimed to answer the questions: Why are young adults, the most diverse generations in America, so difficult to reach by the traditional mainline church? What can we do about it? And, how can we make ministry more effective?

In sections one and two, we looked at the "old rules" of mature generations (Traditionalists, Boomers, and Generation X) and contrasted them with the "new rules" of Millennials and Generation Z while shattering the myth that generations are monolithic. In fact, we've come to understand that demographics are fluid and lifestyles are constantly changing within and across generations.

In section three, we highlighted some of our favorite innovative organizations in the United States (Facebook, Starbucks, Uber, Netflix, and Disney) that are demonstrating deep understanding, relational ability, and impact with younger generations. Millennials are the least churched adult generation and the least likely either to identify as Christian or say faith is very important to their life.[1] As a result, looking outside the church for understanding and effective strategy is essential.

In section four, we invited you into a blank slate using design thinking as a model to create innovative solutions to problems while putting the people you're trying to reach at the center. In particular, we emphasized that design thinking is all about creating remarkable experiences with Millennials and Generation Z at the center because these are the younger generations we seek to reach. With this blank slate, the kind of action for which we're calling is a new kind of spiritual leadership that reaches across generations, lifestyles, and cultures. Importantly, this kind of leadership is the call of every person, not just religious professionals. In the role of spiritual leader a person chooses to be immersed in the world and in God. She loves humanity and Jesus. He seeks diverse relationships with people and deliberately takes time away from people to be with God. This leader is led by a deep knowing that the pandemonium of life does not have the last word. This new spiritual leader realizes that we are courageously living in between times of sadness and joy, turmoil and peace, disbelief and eternal hope. At their best, spiritual leaders bear their souls through the sharing of personal struggles so others may see the enduring qualities of God, experience courage, and remain hopeful despite their circumstances.

Finally, in section five we shared four important topics for further thinking given the increasing cultural diversity in the United States and around the world: interfaith and multigenerational dialogue, missions, atonement, and reconciliation. We included this section because effective leadership today and into the twenty-second century requires a deeper understanding of gender, racial, economic, and lifestyle diversity more than ever before. No longer will broad generalizations about people who appear different from our experienced norms suffice.

Regardless of the type of industry or organization there are common ingredients that attract and keep younger generations involved. The desire to belong to organizations where their opinions are respected and they can relate to the mission from their unique vantage point is essential. Contrary to popular stereotypes that Millennials are hard to get along with, organizations that desire to connect with younger people are learning the benefits of reverse mentoring.

Younger team members previously sidelined as secondary idea producers are now valued as first-line creatives who are able to anticipate trends, thoughts, and upcoming desires of their peers. Older leaders are realizing the benefits of having those voices at the table because they bring to discussions fresh insight and thinking that is deeply rooted in "the experience" of the end user.

Even growing churches have abandoned the words "worship service" and now use the preferred term, "worship experience." It is the user experience that frames the relevance and value of the product and practice being offered. The anchoring question is, "What's in this for me?". It is at the heart of marketing, engagement, and interest. These younger generations bring a multi-layered thought process to the presentation, style, and use of the end-user experience.

In past generations the focus has been on sustainability or building on a single theme, whereas today's focus is on anticipating changing trends that speak to the evolving relevance of a product or experience. A good example of this is car commercials. They are completely aimed at the user experience. The commercials are geared to speak to our heartfelt reactions, inviting us to experience the product.

This is not to say that these younger generations don't provide substance. On the contrary, they are able to harness the entirety of their senses so that the user experience is a full-sensory event. While older generations have anchored their sales pitches in what's the value, younger generations ask, "How does this experience make me feel better about myself?"

This incorporation of younger mindsets is helping to define everything from home delivery services to mobile communications that make our lives easier. The growing discussion regarding artificial intelligence is anchored in the thoughts of these new generations of folks who are very comfortable allowing machines to anticipate, automate, and shape the ways we do life together. The evolution of the handheld device from being primarily a phone to being an all-inclusive control system is evidence of the influence of new generations thinking beyond the limitations of the past.

This team approach to creation and leadership is anchoring a movement toward a broader team approach to implementation of fresh approaches to design and usability. At the heart of this movement is an emerging shared awareness that long-time norms in the workplace and society are being replaced with changing and sometimes challenging encounters. At the heart of these changes is a common link of relevance and respect. A review of an issue of *Fortune, Oprah, Fast Company*, and *Black Enterprise* magazines reveals the growing number of younger thought leaders who are revolutionizing various industries. They are revolutionizing everything from new techniques for development to new ways of repurposing existing products.

This redesign and realignment of collaborative teaming are creating new methods of ideation and presentation. We see this in the rising number of younger creatives who see themselves as artists. These processes are seen in the creation of worship design teams, outside collaborators, and the integration of cross-cultural and cross-generational experiences. While Uber and Lyft are trending for young people today, they are on the cutting edge of a future normal transportation system for seniors who no longer want to drive. This will be followed shortly by self-driving transportation, already well under development. The integration of Amazon and Whole Foods is an example of how home delivery will soon overtake shopping not only for groceries but also for clothing, household items, prescription medicines, and many other things in our lives.

So where do we go from here?

It is interesting how younger generations connect. They use technology to promote and rebrand themselves, they gather in informal and formal networks to market themselves, and they learn from one another. They see themselves as important links to an evolving product just waiting to be asked to join the team. Unlike their parents and grandparents, they don't see themselves working on a job for a long time, rather they see themselves as nomads traveling through life making contributions and moving forward to the next place where they can share their gifts and talents. What older generations see as instability is a new culture of building one's skill set through ever challenging encounters and experiences.

Being a part of something new, becoming a part of something that will "change the world," is a significant part of self-discovery and human worth. This job shifting also builds achievements and creates new levels of competence and self-development. This career movement is the new higher education certification. So much so that some young people are skipping traditional college careers to immerse themselves into creative cohorts that assist them to build phenomenal resumes.

Rebranding, pivoting, and other methods of transformation often leads to a leap of faith that develops into something really significant. Books like John Maxwell's *No Limits: Blow the Cap Off Your Capacity*; Jenny Blake's *Pivot: The Only Move You Make Is Your Next One*; and Tim Harford's *Messy: The Power of Disorder to*

Transform Our Lives speak to this reality. What all these resources have in common is a pathway to an evolution of the way generations live into the future with bold and courageous outlooks and attitudes.

At the time of the writing of this book, *Fast Company* made a list of some incredible creative people in business for 2018. Among them are five students from Marjory Stoneman Douglas High School whose advocacy and passion around gun-control has ignited a new generation of courageous thinkers and doers. Creating community and focusing people around a cause is shaping an entirely new way of bringing people together to change and create.

The epiphany that these younger generations are launching is a renewed interest in building systems and networks that utilize known parts and bring them together to build new second- and third-generation applications. New designs are not just for buildings, they are for implementing game changing strategies in all aspects of our lives.

The change for older generations is to free up newer creatives so they are not confined to living in the old structures of our organizations, and to free them up to see beyond the present, to craft innovations, and to empower them to develop new cultural "norms." It has been said that the things that attract younger workers to companies are a sense that they are valued, the company having a clear mission that changes something for the good, work-life balance, a focus on the environment, shared values, social involvement, a collaborative culture, and chances to do something new.

Cultures with multigenerational employees will have the experience of older workers and the edginess of the younger workers, the dedication of the older workers and the collaboration of the younger workers. The key is to create opportunities for cross-generational coaching and mentoring. Baby Boomers, Gen Xers, and Millennials share some common desires for working together. They value chances for advancement, opportunities to learn and grow, and cultures that align with life goals.

Finally, while we have not addressed the changing political climate in the United States and its impact on the church, culture, and our communities in this writing, it is of utmost importance and deserves serious reflection. In alignment with the theme of this book we cannot ignore the impact of how twenty-eight-year-old Alexandria Ocasio-Cortez, a Democratic Socialist from New York, just pulled off a big political upset in 2018. She defeated Representative Joe Crowley (D-N.Y.), who lost his seat to the progressive political newcomer on Tuesday, June 26, 2018. Her upset by 58 percent of the vote over the long-time incumbent, who received just 42 percent of the vote, is a sign of things to come. A compelling message, a compelling organization, an effective social media strategy, and a strong network of grass-root supporters are signs that younger generations are no long willing to wait "until it's their turn." Ocasio-Cortez represents a generation of Millennials who are harnessing their abilities and shaping the future in every aspect of our lives.

There is a change in the air fueled by new generations of people who are now aware that they have the skills, networks, and resources to bring about change. The old rules are being thrown out and new the rules are being shaped while we are in the midst of writing this resource. By the time this publication reaches you, bloggers, podcasters, social media enthusiasts, and others using new forms of message evangelism will have crafted new thoughts, disciples, and new behaviors.

How will you proactively create your blank slate?

NOTES

Introduction

1. http://www.pewforum.org/2015/05/12/americas-changing-religious-landscape/ (accessed June 21, 2018).

2. James Emery White, *Meet Generation Z: Understanding and Reaching the New Post-Christian World*.

3. https://youtu.be/389RR-DjB4g, (November 6, 2014).

4. http://www.gcfa.org/gcfa/data-services-statistics

5. *Thoughts Upon Methodism*, XIII: 258

6. http://missioninsite.com/our-solutions/faithconnect/data-sets

7. http://missioninsite.com/

8. https://www.barna.com/research/meet-love-jesus-not-church/

9. "Tabula Rasa." Merriam-Webster.com. *Merriam-Webster*, n.d. Web. 21 June 2018.

10. Ephesians 4:20-24 (MSG), http://bible.com/97/eph.4.20-24.msg

11. The increasingly diverse United States of America The racial and ethnic diversity of communities varies greatly across the country, but rapid change is coming to many of the least-diverse areas. https://www.washingtonpost.com/graphics/national/how-diverse-is-america/, accessed March 21, 2018.

12. Thomas G. Bandy, *Spiritual Leadership: Why Leaders Lead and Who Seekers Seek to Follow* (Nashville: Abingdon, 2016), 16.

13. The UNESCO World Report No. 2: Investing in Cultural Diversity and Intercultural Dialogue (ISBN 978-92-3-104077-1), www.unesco.org/en/world-reports/cultural-diversity.

1. Old Rules of the Traditionalists

1. https://kinginstitute.stanford.edu/king-papers/publications /autobiography-martin-luther-king-jr-contents/chapter-1-early -years

2. https://kinginstitute.stanford.edu/king-papers/publications /autobiography-martin-luther-king-jr-contents/chapter-1-early -years

3. https://www.nationalww2museum.org/sites/default/files /2017-07/african-americans.pdf

4. Statement by the President; 5/22/1950; May 22, 1950—(Final Meeting with President); Meetings Files, 1948–1950; Records of Temporary Committees, Commissions, and Boards, Record Group 220; Harry S. Truman Library, Independence, MO (online version, https://www.docsteach.org/documents/document /statement-president-truman, March 21, 2018).

5. https://livinghistoryfarm.org/farminginthe40s/life_18.html

6. http://www.thearda.com/Denoms/D_1432.asp

7. Robert P. Jones, *The End of White Christian America*.

8. Ibid.

9. Ibid.

2. Old Rules of the Boomers

1. https://www.census.gov/prod/2014pubs/p25-1141.pdf (accessed May 14, 2018).

2. https://www.ourdocuments.gov/doc.php?flash=false&doc=97

3. http://americanarchive.org/exhibits/first-amendment /protests-60s-70s (accessed May 14, 2018).

4. Ibid.

5. http://www.notablebiographies.com/We-Z/Winfrey -Oprah.html (accessed May 14, 2018).

6. https://www.eduinreview.com/blog/2011/02/oprah-win freys-education-background/ (accessed January 16, 2019).

7. https://youtu.be/-nCb6ALDtng (accessed May 14, 2018).

8. https://youtu.be/nDXnFZMa7mU (accessed May 14, 2018).

9. https://www.census.gov/prod/2014pubs/p25-1141.pdf (accessed May 14, 2018).

10. Craig Miller, https://boomerspirituality.org/miller-presentations/ (accessed May 14, 2018).

3. Old Rules of Generation Xers

1. http://www.pewresearch.org/fact-tank/2018/03/01/defining-generations-where-millennials-end-and-post-millennials-begin/ (accessed May 29, 2018).

2. http://www.pewresearch.org/fact-tank/2014/06/05/generation-x-americas-neglected-middle-child/

3. http://www.bbc.com/culture/story/20170316-whatever-happened-to-generation-x (accessed August 31, 2018).

4. https://www.cnbc.com/2018/04/11/generation-x-not-millennials-is-changing-the-nature-of-work.html (accessed on August 31, 2018).

5. https://www.fastcompany.com/40558008/why-you-need-to-pay-attention-to-gen-x-leaders (accessed August 31, 2018).

6. http://www.pewsocialtrends.org/2018/04/25/the-changing-profile-of-unmarried-parents/ (accessed May 15, 2018).

7. http://www.pewforum.org/2015/11/03/u-s-public-becoming-less-religious/

8. http://www.pewresearch.org/fact-tank/2017/09/06/more-americans-now-say-theyre-spiritual-but-not-religious/

9. http://www.pewforum.org/religious-landscape-study/generational-cohort/ (accessed May 16, 2018).

4. New Rules of Millennials

1. https://www.barna.com/research/when-millennials-go-to-work/

2. https://www.beloit.edu/mindset/previouslists/2002/

3. https://www.federalreserve.gov/publications/2017
-economic-well-being-of-us-households-in-2016-education
-debt-loans.htm

4. UMC School of Congregational Development, "Empowering Millennials through Arts and Activism" Workshop, August 16, 2018.

5. https://www.fastcompany.com/40587156/these-are-the
-ceos-most-employees-want-to-work-for (accessed June 28, 2018).

6. https://www.bls.gov/news.release/empsit.nr0.htm

7. https://www.barna.com/research/meet-love-jesus-not
-church/

8. https://www.barna.com/research/americans-divided-on
-the-importance-of-church/

9. https://www.cnn.com/2015/05/12/living/pew-religion
-study/index.html

10. http://www.pewforum.org/2015/05/12/americas-changing
-religious-landscape/

11. http://www.pewresearch.org/fact-tank/2015/05/13/a
-closer-look-at-americas-rapidly-growing-religious-nones/

12. UMC School of Congregational Development, "Empowering Millennials through Arts and Activism" Workshop, August 16, 2018.

13. https://www.businessinsider.com/xennials-born-between
-millennials-and-gen-x-2017-11#this-group-has-also-been-called
-the-oregon-trail-generation-in-reference-to-a-popular-computer
-game-when-they-were-growing-up-2 (accessed August 31, 2018).

14. https://www.churchleadership.com/leading-ideas/when
-a-pastor-serves-a-church-of-a-different-racial-or-cultural-back
ground/

5. New Rules of Generation Z

1. http://www.pewresearch.org/fact-tank/2018/03/01/defining
-generations-where-millennials-end-and-post-millennials-begin/
(accessed May 29, 2018).

2. "Innovation Imperative: Meet Generation Z," Northeastern University, http://www.northeastern.edu/news/2014/11/innovation-imperative-meet-generation-z/.

3. http://projectchangetheworld.weebly.com/home.html (accessed July 2, 2018).

4. "Innovation Imperative: Meet Generation Z," Northeastern University, http://www.northeastern.edu/news/2014/11/innovation-imperative-meet-generation-z/.

5. David Freed and Idrees Kahloon, "Beliefs and Lifestyle," Harvard Crimson, http://features.thecrimson.com/2015/freshman-survey/lifestyle/.

6. "Meet Generation Z," Sparks and Honey.

Section 3. Lessons from Innovative Organization

1. https://www.barna.com/research/meet-love-jesus-not-church/

6. Facebook

1. http://www.businessinsider.com/how-facebook-was-founded-2010-3

2. https://www.prnewswire.com/news-releases/facebook-reports-fourth-quarter-and-full-year-2017-results-300591468.html (accessed May 4, 2018).

3. eMarketer, and Squarespace. Number of Facebook users by age in the U.S. as of January 2018 (in millions). https://www.statista.com/statistics/398136/us-facebook-user-age-groups/ (accessed May 4, 2018).

4. eMarketer. Average daily time spent on selected social networks by users in the United States from 2014 to 2019 (in minutes). https://www.statista.com/statistics/324290/us-users-daily-facebook-minutes/ (accessed May 4, 2018).

5. *Harvard Business Review.* "What are the top three companies you want to work for?" https://www.statista.com

/statistics/292597/companies-us-millennials-work/ (accessed May 4, 2018).

6. Mark Zuckerberg, "How to Build the Future," YouTube, August 16, 2016, https://youtu.be/Lb4IcGF5iTQ (accessed May 4, 2018).

7. Ibid.

8. www.shrm.org/resourcesandtools/hr-topics/behavioral -competencies/global-and-cultural-effectiveness/pages/millennial -impact.aspx (accessed August 25, 2018).

9. www.worklearning.com/2006/05/01/people_remember/ (accessed August 25, 2018).

10. http://newsroom.fb.com/news/2017/06/our-first-com-munities-summit-and-new-tools-for-group-admins/ (accessed August 25, 2018).

7. Starbucks

1. Howard Schultz and Joanne Gordon, *Onward: How Star-bucks Fought for Its Life without Losing Its Soul* (NY: Rodale, 2011), 3.

2. https://www.statista.com/statistics/266465/number-of -starbucks-stores-worldwide/

3. https://www.starbucks.com/ (accessed, May 29, 2018).

4. https://www.nytimes.com/2018/05/29/business/star bucks-closing-racial-bias-training.html (accessed May 29, 2018).

5. Ibid.

6. Schultz, *Onward*, 59.

7. Ibid., 106.

8. Ibid.

9. Ibid., 108.

10. https://www.nytimes.com/roomfordebate/2014/04/13 /the-pros-and-cons-of-gentrification/every-community-deserves -a-third-place (accessed May 29, 2018).

11. https://www.brookings.edu/blog/up-front/2016/09/14 /third-places-as-community-builders/ (accessed May 29, 2018).

8. Uber

1.   https://www.washingtonpost.com/news/theworldpost /wp/2018/02/01/uber-economy/ (accessed June 28, 2008).

2.   https://nypost.com/2017/07/15/this-minister-turned-his -uber-car-into-a-church-on-wheels/ (accessed June 28, 2018).

3.   https://www.uber.com/newsroom/company-info/   (accessed June 28, 2018).

4.   https://www.uber.com/newsroom/driving-change-by-con necting-with-the-communities-we-serve/ (accessed June 28, 2018).

5.   https://www.uber.com/newsroom/driving-change-by-con necting-with-the-communities-we-serve/ (accessed June 28, 2018).

6.   https://www.uber.com/newsroom/getting-serious-safety/ (accessed June 28, 2018).

7. https://www.uber.com/newsroom/uber-health/ (accessed June 28, 2018).

8. Ibid.

9. Netflix

1. https://www.fastcompany.com/company/netflix (accessed June 29, 2018).

2. https://www.cnbc.com/2017/05/23/netflix-ceo-reed-hastings -on-how-the-company-was-born.html (accessed June 29, 2018).

3.   https://www.facebook.com/pg/netflixus/about/?ref=page _internal (accessed June 29, 2018).

4.   https://www.bt.com.au/personal/your-goals/your-well being/your-financial-health/5-things-netflix-can-teach-us-about -innovation.html (accessed June 29, 2018).

5. Ibid.

6. https://youtu.be/OeyxR8WJiaI (accessed June 29, 2018).

7. https://variety.com/2018/tv/news/netflix-black-great-day -in-harlem-image-spot-1202856238/ (accessed June 29, 2018).

8. https://variety.com/2018/tv/news/netflix-black-great-day -in-harlem-image-spot-1202856238/ (accessed June 29, 2018).

10. A Disney Experience

1. https://www.airbnb.com/ (accessed June 12, 2018).

2. https://www.uber.com/newsroom/company-info/ (accessed June 12, 2018).

3. www.disneyatwork.com (2018).

Section 4. Creating New Models of Ministry

1. http://www.designkit.org/human-centered-design (accessed August 27, 2018).

2. "Tabula Rasa," Merriam-Webster.com, Web. 21 June 2018.

3. https://hbr.org/1998/07/welcome-to-the-experience-economy (accessed June 12, 2018).

4. https://www.umcdiscipleship.org/new-church-starts/mission-possible-design-thinking-for-social-change (accessed June 21, 2018).

Game Time!

1. https://www.umcdiscipleship.org/new-church-starts/mission-possible-design-thinking-for-social-change (accessed June 21, 2018).

2. A. L. Hammer and E. R. Schnell, FIRO-B Technical Guide (Mountain View, CA: CPP, 2000).

3. Ibid.

4. http://www.pewresearch.org/fact-tank/2017/01/04/5-facts-about-the-minimum-wage/ (accessed June 21, 2018).

5. http://www.pewresearch.org/fact-tank/2016/09/01/8-facts-about-american-workers/ (accessed June, 21, 2018).

6. https://www.census.gov/library/publications/2017/demo/p60-260.html (accessed June 22, 2018).

7. http://www.childrensdefense.org/library/PovertyReport/EndingChildPovertyNow.html (accessed June 24, 2018).

8. Ending Child Poverty Now, http://www.childrensdefense
.org/ (accessed June 24, 2018).

9. http://www.childrensdefense.org/library/PovertyReport
/EndingChildPovertyNow.html (accessed June 24, 2018).

10. http://www.umc.org/what-we-believe/economic
-community (accessed June 24, 2018).

11. Thomas Lockwood, *Design Thinking* (New York: All-worth, 2009), 114.

12. Ibid., 115.

13. The Field Guide to Human-Centered Design By IDEO
.org, 1st Edition © 2015, ISBN: 978-0-9914063-1-9

11. Seven Mindsets and Actions to Create Your Own Blank Slate

1. *The Bicentennial Edition of the Works of John Wesley*, 9:256–57.

2. Ibid., 9:266–67.

3. Ibid., 77–78.

4. Ibid., 9:261.

5. "Story," *Dictionary of Feminist Theologies*, ed. Letty M. Russell and Shannon J. Clarkson, 278.

6. "Empowerment," *Dictionary of Feminist Theologies*, 86.

7. www.ministrymatters.com/all/entry/6034/belonging (accessed May 24, 2018).

8. "Faith," *Dictionary of Feminist Theologies*, 96.

9. http://bible.com/111/1co.10.16-17.niv (accessed June 28, 2018).

10. Letty M. Russell, *Dictionary of Feminist Theologies*, 201.

11. Henry H. Mitchell, *Black Church Beginnings: The Long-Hidden Realities of the First Years* (Grand Rapids: Eerdmans, 2004), 162.

12. C. Eric Lincoln and Lawrence H. Mamiya, *The Black Church in the African American Experience* (Durham, NC: Duke University Press, 1990), 251.

13. Randall M. Miller and John David Smith, editors, *Dictionary of Afro-American Slavery* (New York: Greenwood, 1988), 209.

14. Ibid., 212.

15. Ibid.

16. Mitchell, 142.

17. Harry A. Ploski and James Williams, editors, *Reference Library of Black America* (Philadelphia: Afro-American Press, 1990), 735.

18. Mitchell, 143.

19. Ibid., 145.

20. Ibid., 146–47.

21. Lincoln & Mamiya, 252

22. Mitchell, 156.

23. Lincoln & Mamiya, 172

24. Ibid., 171.

25. J. Deotis Roberts, *Afrocentric Christianity: A Theological Appraisal for Ministry* (Valley Forge, PA: Judson, 2000), 60.

Section 5. Topics for Further Thinking

1. The increasingly diverse United States of America. The racial and ethnic diversity of communities varies greatly across the country, but rapid change is coming to many of the least-diverse areas. https://www.washingtonpost.com/graphics/national/how-diverse-is-america/ (accessed March 21, 2018).

2. Thomas G Bandy, *Spiritual Leadership: Why Leaders Lead and Who Seekers Follow* (Nashville: Abingdon, 2016), 16.

3. The UNESCO World Report No. 2: Investing in Cultural Diversity and Intercultural Dialogue (ISBN 978-92-3-104077-1), www.unesco.org/en/world-reports/cultural-diversity.

12. Interfaith and Intergenerational Dialogue

1. Raimon Panikkar, "Ramon Panikkar and the Unknown Christ," in *Christ in Evolution*, Ilia Delia (Maryknoll, NY: Orbis Books, 2008), 84.

2. Ibid., 85–86.

3. Karen Baker-Fletcher, "Difference," *Dictionary of Feminist Theologies*, Letty Russell and J. Shannon Clarkson, eds. (Louisville: Westminster John Knox Press, 1996), 68.

4. F. Douglas Powe, CHS 340 class lecture "Enlightenment Project" (Kansas City: The Saint Paul School of Theology, Sept. 2009).

5. Panikkar, 87.

6. Ibid., 93.

7. Paula M. Cooey, "Pluralism: Theological Responses," *Dictionary of Feminist Theologies*, Letty Russell and J. Shannon Clarkson, eds. (Louisville: Westminster John Knox , 1996), 211.

8. Panikkar, 96–97.

9. Ranya Idliby, Suzanne Oliver, and Priscilla Warner, *The Faith Club* (New York: Free Press, 2006), 353–56.

10. Letty M. Russell, "Partnership" *Dictionary of Feminist Theologies*, Letty Russell and J. Shannon Clarkson, eds. (Louisville: Westminster John Knox, 1996), 201.

11. Ilia Delia, *Christ in Evolution* (Maryknoll, NY: Orbis, 2008), 102.

12. Adair T. Lummis, "Pluralism, Religious," *Dictionary of Feminist Theologies*, Letty Russell and J. Shannon Clarkson, eds. (Louisville: Westminster John Knox, 1996), 210.

13. Ubuntu

1. Dirk J. Louw, "Ubuntu: An African Assessment of the Religious Other" in *Philosophy in Africa*, http://www.bu.edu/wcp /Papers/Afri/AfriLouw.htm (accessed April 27, 2010).

2. Ibid.

3. Ibid.

4. Ibid.

5. Donald K. McKim, "Mission" in *Westminster Dictionary of Theological Terms* (Louisville: Westminster John Knox, 1996), 175.

6. Dr. Rena Yocum, MIN 422 class lecture (Kansas City: The Saint Paul School of Theology, 3 Feb. 2010).

7. Donald K. McKim, "Apostle" in *Westminster Dictionary of Theological Terms* (Louisville: Westminster John Knox, 1996), 15.

8. "Liberation," United Communities of Spirit, http://origin .org/ucs/ws/theme070.cfm (accessed April 26, 2010).

9. Ken Gnanakan, "To Proclaim the Good News of the Kingdom" Andrew Walls and Cathy Ross, eds. *Mission in the 21st Century: Exploring the Five Marks of Global Mission* (Maryknoll, NY: Orbis, 2008), 6.

10. Vauadi Vibila, "Marginalization" in *Dictionary of Feminist Theologies*, Letty M. Russell and J. Shannon Clarkson, eds. (Louisville: Westminster John Knox, 1996), 170.

11. Maulana Karenga, "Principles and Practices of Kwanzaa: Repairing and Renewing the World" http://www.official kwanzaawebsite.org/documents/PrinciplesandPracticesof Kwanzaa_000.pdf (accessed April 18, 2010).

12. Michael L. Cook, "Yield Not to Temptation: Confronting the Financial Challenges of the Black Family" *Multidimensional Ministry for Today's Black Family*, Johnny B. Hill, ed. (Valley Forge, PA: Judson, 2007), 76.

13. Chris Haslam, Revised Common Lectionary Commentary, http://montreal.anglican.org/comments/archive/cpr03l.shtml (accessed April 26, 2010).

14. Sherrill McMillan, "Elephants in the Pews: Confronting Silent Issues in the Church" *Multidimensional Ministry for Today's Black Family*, Johnny B. Hill, ed. (Valley Forge, PA: Judson, 2007), 15–25.

15. Samuel O. Abogunrin "Jesus' Sevenfold Programmatic Declaration at Nazareth: An Exegesis from an African Perspective," *Black Theology: An International Journal* (1.2 2001), 234.

16. Ibid., 225–49.

17. Karenga, "Principles and Practices."

18. Johnny B. Hill, ed. *Multidimensional Ministry for Today's Black Family* (Valley Forge, PA: Judson, 2007), 1–13.

19. Ibid., 59.

20. Brian Stoffregen, http://www.crossmarks.com/brian /luke4x14.htm (accessed April 26, 2010).

21. Marvin A. McMickle, *Preaching to the Black Middle Class: Words of Challenge, Words of Hope* (Valley Forge, PA: Judson, 2000), 9.

22. Donald E. Messer, *Contemporary Images of Christian Ministry* (Nashville: Abingdon, 1989), 141.

23. Cone, 8.

14. Intergenerational and Multicultural Atonement, Reconciliation, and Peace

1. https://www.cnn.com/specials/weather/hurricane-maria (accessed July 1, 2018).

2. Thomas F. Torrance, *Atonement: The Person and Work of Christ* (Colorado Springs: InterVarsity, 2009), 137.

3. Ibid.

4. Eugene Teselle, "Atonement," *A New Handbook of Christian Theology*, Donald W. Messer and Joseph L. Price, eds. (Nashville: Abingdon, 1992), 41.

5. Teselle, 42.

6. Donald K. McKim, "Atonement," *Westminster Dictionary of Theological Terms* (Louisville: Westminster John Knox, 1996), 20.

7. Ibid.

8. Delores S. Williams, "Atonement," *Dictionary of Feminist Theologies* (Louisville: Westminster John Knox, 1996), 18.

9. Delores S. Williams, *Sisters in the Wilderness* (Maryknoll, NY: Orbis, 1993), 164.

10. Linda J. Vogel, "Reconciliation," *An A to Z of Feminist Theology*, Lisa Isherwood and Dorothea McEwan, eds. (Sheffield, England: Sheffield Academic, 1996), 197.

11. Ibid.
12. Ibid.
13. Torrance, 170.

Conclusion

1. https://www.barna.com/research/meet-love-jesus-not-church/

CPSIA information can be obtained
at www.ICGtesting.com
Printed in the USA
LVHW030332080519
617006LV00004BA/5/P

9 781501 876264